The
New
Forest

A Personal View by C.A. Brebbia

The New Forest

A Personal View by C.A. Brebbia

WITPRESS Southampton, Boston

C.A. Brebbia
Wessex Institute of Technology

Published by

WIT Press

Ashurst Lodge, Ashurst, Southampton, SO40 7AA, UK
Tel: 44 (0) 238 029 3223; Fax: 44 (0) 238 029 2853
E-Mail: witpress@witpress.com
http://www.witpress.com

For USA, Canada and Mexico

WIT Press

25 Bridge Street, Billerica, MA 01821, USA
Tel: 978 667 5841; Fax: 978 667 7582
E-Mail: infousa@witpress.com
http://www.witpress.com

British Library Cataloguing-in-Publication Data

A Catalogue record for this book is available
from the British Library

ISBN: 978-1-84564-145-0

Library of Congress Catalog Card Number: 2008924942

CONTENTS

ACKNOWLEDGEMENTS

This book was written with the help and collaboration of many people.

Most of the photographs in the volume were taken by my friend and colleague Pier Paolo Strona and by our Institute graphic designer, Keith Godwin, both of whom undertook the task as a labour of love, prompted in Keith's case by his family association with the locality and in Pier Paolo's by the unique and aesthetic appeal of the New Forest. Their photographs greatly enhance this new edition.

Brian Privett, the Head of Production at WIT Press, oversaw the whole publishing process in his highly professional manner, supervising the work of sub-editors and graphic artists and the final printing.

I am grateful to Eric Smith for his expert editing of my manuscript and to Isabelle Strafford who patiently tidied up the final version. Brian Green's excellent sense of design and typography helped to make the book much easier to read.

Many others have contributed including some local people who shared their knowledge and anecdotes about the New Forest in general and Ashurst Lodge in particular. I am especially indebted to Richard Reeves, librarian at the New Forest Museum, for helping provide me with information on the history of Ashurst Lodge. His careful research reflects his deep knowledge of the Forest.

Foremost amongst my collaborators is my wife, Carolyn, who helped me research the history of our home here in the New Forest.

Carlos A. Brebbia
The New Forest, 2008

LIST OF ILLUSTRATIONS

PREFACE

When I first came to Southampton many years ago, I was immediately impressed by the beauty and history of the New Forest. Very different from many other national parks in Britain and other places around the world, the New Forest is home to a large number of people and this makes it a more dynamic environment.

Since the 11th century, the New Forest has continued to develop and change without losing its unique ambience. It has been a royal hunting ground, a source of timber to the nation, an area for grazing cattle, a producer of minerals and charcoal and, more recently, a place dedicated to leisure activities. The different uses of the Forest have generated numerous industries: since Roman times it has been renowned for its pottery and more, recently, industries as varied as shipbuilding and gunpowder manufacture have taken place in the Forest.

Because of the diversity of uses and ever-changing activities in the Forest, it did not appear to be a contradiction to establish an institute of advanced studies in the midst of the Forest, and we moved our development and research here in 1982, where the quiet and pleasant environment was conducive to our activities. It is indeed difficult to think of a better place for intellectual work and especially for research.

After having moved our Institute to the Forest, I later realised my ambition of living in the Forest by purchasing a property in Burley. Since then I have had the privilege of both living and working in the New Forest, which has led me to appreciate better its history and amenities.

I appreciate that in spite of my commitment I shall never become a true Forester, but I hope to help preserve the environment for future generations and in a modest way make a positive contribution to the New Forest, which has now become a National Park in recognition of its unique value to the nation.

I have not attempted to discuss all parts of the Forest or all historical events in this book. It is mainly a personal view, highlighting places and stories that will be of interest to a wide audience.

I hope that the reader will enjoy my personal view of the New Forest.

Carlos A. Brebbia

Arms of
Wessex Institute of
Technology

Tempora mutantur nos
mutamur in illis

CARLOS A. BREBBIA
Director and Founder of Wessex Institute of Technology

INTRODUCTION

Welcome to the New Forest and in particular to Ashurst Lodge, home of the Wessex Institute of Technology and the Computational Mechanics International group of companies. This group comprises the company marketing the Boundary Element Analysis Code, BEASY, as well as the academic publishers, WIT Press. It also operates as a property company specialising in heritage buildings.

Ashurst Lodge itself is a property of architectural interest, situated in the New Forest, now a National Park. The Lodge is convenient for the centre of Southampton – approximately 6 miles (10 km) away. It is easy to reach by road on the M3 motorway from London, which connects with the M27 motorway. The Lodge is served by three important airports: Heathrow, approximately one hour's drive away; Southampton Airport approximately 10 miles (16 km) on the M27; and the airport at Bournemouth, Christchurch, which is situated just west of the New Forest. Gatwick Airport is more distant at over one hour by car.

Southampton can be reached by train from London's Waterloo station, the journey taking about an hour.

Ashurst village has its own train station, a mile or so from the Lodge. This is on the main London–Southampton–Bournemouth line, and trains to and from Waterloo stop there. The station, called 'Ashurst New Forest', is better served by local trains going to and from Southampton.

I hope that you will enjoy the Forest; in my opinion our unique working environment has contributed in great part to the excellence of our research and advanced engineering activities. The intention of this book – now in its fifth printing – is to give you some idea of our environment so that you will be able to share our feelings for this part of England.

John Wise was one of the 19th-century writers who took an interest in the Forest and, in his 1862 book on its history and scenery, wrote the following prophetic words:

> The time will someday arrive when as England becomes more and more overcrowded – as each heath and common are swallowed up – the New Forest will be as much a necessity to the country as the parks are now to London.

I think that that time has now come.

Carlos A. Brebbia

A BIT OF HISTORY

The New Forest before the Normans

The New Forest, or Nova Foresta to give it its old title, was so designated in the late 11th century, by the first Norman king of England, William I or 'the Conqueror', on land that was too poor for agricultural exploitation but provided good hunting ground.

Although a large number of ancient burial barrows still exist – most of them dating from the Bronze Age – the Forest appears to have always been sparsely populated. Many barrows contain cremation urns as well as other artefacts and pottery of the period. The famous author Sir Walter Scott excavated some of these barrows but did not leave a record of what he found. John Wise inspected others and reported that they contained charcoal and burnt earth amongst which were calcinated bones. Some of them contained Celtic urns, while more recent ones had Roman-type pottery.

An excellent example of an Iron Age fort construction is Castle Hill near my house in Burley. This is a hill-top fort giving a wide-ranging view of the surrounding countryside. The original ditches and foundations of the fence encircling the fort can still be clearly seen. The function of this fort was probably to act as an enclosure where animals could be kept during the night and where people could defend themselves against attack.

There are many other prehistoric earthworks in the Forest, including a circular hill fort 400 m or so south of Ashurst Lodge. It consists of a mound 11 m in diameter and almost 1 m in height, surrounded by a rampart and an external ditch. This type of earthwork dates from between the late Bronze Age and the Early Iron Age (8th–5th centuries BC). They contained round houses and granaries.

Part of a circular earthwork near Ashurst Lodge of 80m in diameter and surrounded with a bank and a ditch. *[photo by Keith Godwin]*

The ancient inhabitants of the Forest were Celts. The Roman conquest in Gaul displaced some of the Belgae tribes on the Continent and they crossed the Channel to establish themselves in modern Sussex in the 1st century bc. Over the next century they moved westwards into Hampshire and the New Forest where they were settled by the time the Romans invaded Britain. Although no important Roman villas have been discovered in the Forest, some traces of their roads were found. A Roman road started from the mouth of the estuary of the Beaulieu River and Exbury and progressed north, indicating that the maritime trade through the Forest may have been larger than previously estimated. Another Roman road entered the Forest from the east up to Stoney Cross, where it ends in a sort of T-junction. These roads were used to transport tin from Cornwall and lead from other mines. The only Roman fort in the New Forest district was situated at St Catherine's Hill, north-west of Christchurch, where the

Romans kept a small garrison.

The main industry of the Forest in those times may have been pottery, of which the Romans used vast quantities. There were then numerous kilns in the Forest, as pointed out by Heywood Sumner, and although they were small and did not seem to stimulate any settlement around them, New Forest pottery was used throughout Britain.

After the Romans left, the Jutes settled in the Forest and they were there when the Saxon invasion took place. According to the Anglo-Saxon Chronicle, this happened on the west side of Southampton Water, probably in what is now Fawley, at around AD 500.

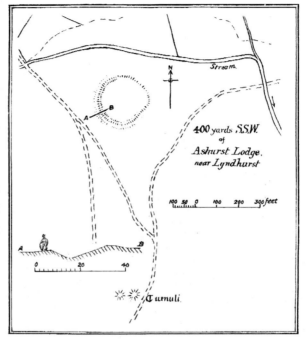

Circular Entrenchement or 'fort' located south of Ashurst Lodge, consisting of a low bank and ditch. There are two barrows 200 metres to the south of this 'fort' (after Williams-Freeman).

The remains of an extensive Saxon settlement have been discovered in Southampton, though it was Winchester that became the capital of the kingdom of Wessex – West Saxons – and was, for a time, the capital of England.

The Normans and Afterwards

In 1066 the Normans invaded England and William the Conqueror decided soon afterwards to establish a New Forest near Winchester, where he had been crowned and the Treasury was kept. It was also at Winchester that the Domesday Book was compiled. Undoubtedly a Forest already existed here before, which in

The open forest. *[photo by Pier Paolo Strona]*

the days of Canute was made into a Royal Forest, but in 1079 William I defined its boundary, established the Forest Law and carried out works of afforestation, all to ensure plentiful game and good sport for the royal household.

Tradition and the tales of many Saxon chroniclers state that William laid waste to villages and houses in the Forest, but this is no longer thought to be true. It is now accepted that the stories of the chroniclers were tainted by hatred for the Normans by the defeated.

The extent of the original Forest was much larger than now, comprising the area from Southampton Water and the River Test in the east, to the River Avon in the west and from the sea at Calshot Castle to Christchurch in the south, to the border with Wiltshire in the north. The total area was around 150,000 acres (61,000 ha), compared with the present 90,000 acres (12,000 ha), of which approximately 60,000 (24,000 ha) are now in the hands of the Forestry Commission and 30,000 (12,000 ha) in private hands. Much of the land lost has been eaten away by the development of towns and villages around the periphery, with the resulting encroachments.

William brought his new hunting grounds under the strict regulation of Forest Law. This law, which appears to have originated with Canute, was extremely harsh even for those times. Foresters, those living in the Forest, were given the right to release their animals onto the land and even to cultivate some of it but they could not erect fences or in any way molest or damage the King's animals. Penalties for offences against Forest Law were made even more severe in the time of King Rufus, or William II: he who killed a deer – if of the lower orders – was killed; he who shot at a deer and missed had his hands cut off; and even those who disturbed the deer could have their eyes gouged out!

A peaceful brook in the neighbourhood of Ashurst Lodge. *[photo by Pier Paolo Strona]*

The office of Keeper comes from Canute's laws, where they are called 'Tinemen'. The Domesday Book mentions the office of Keeper of the King's House at Lyndhurst. Much later, when the Office of Woods was set up at the time of William III (1698), the Tinemen became known as 'Keepers'. The Forest by then had been divided into a series of areas called 'walks' and each of them was under the supervision of an under Keeper, who was assigned a residence or 'Lodge', one of which was Ashurst Lodge.

The first son of William I, called Richard, died in the New Forest when chasing a stag. The Domesday Book records that after this incident William returned some lands to their original owners to ensure the repose of his son's soul. A second son of the Conqueror to die in the Forest was his bastard son, also called Richard.

At the death of William the Conqueror, the crown went to his second legitimate surviving son, William Rufus, or 'the Red', rather than to the eldest – Robert, duke of Normandy – who was judged not to be hard enough on the unruly Saxons. Unfortunately Rufus proved to be a bad choice. Full of vices and extremely cruel, he was hated by the Forest people for his rigid enforcement of the Law. The clergy also hated him for not filling vacant ecclesiastic seats, thus pocketing their revenues, leaving vacant even the throne of Canterbury for three years and generally caring little for the Church. He appeared to have been hated by the whole of the country, and eventually died in mysterious circumstances while hunting in the New Forest. A stone encased in cast iron marks the place where he is supposed to have fallen when hit by an arrow shot by one of his courtiers, Sir Walter Tyrrell, perhaps by accident. The hunting party also included Rufus's brother Henry, who with undue haste immediately left for Winchester to claim the crown. Sir Walter galloped away in the opposite direction towards Ringwood and the coast to make his way to Normandy. To this day, a country lane joining Burley Street, near my house, is called Tyrrell's Lane as a reminder of this memorable flight. He crossed the Avon at a spot still called Tyrrell's Ford in an attempt to embark for Normandy from a port other than Lymington or Beaulieu, which were still within the bounds of the Royal Forest. He took a ship from Poole to Normandy and retired to his estates in Picardy. The fact that he left in such a hurry suggests that the deed was perhaps not accidental. Tyrrell's Ford lay on the River Avon between Ringwood and Christchurch. Nearby was a blacksmith's forge, the place where Tyrrell's horse was shod during his flight to Normandy, allegedly with the shoes back to front to mislead any pursuers. In Wise's time, the 1860s, the blacksmith was reportedly still paying each year a fine of three pounds and ten shillings to the Crown for what his predecessor had done.

The suspicions relating to the death of Rufus are reinforced by the haste with which all the protagonists left the scene, leaving behind the body of the king. It was left to a charcoal burner called Purkis to put it on a cart and take it to Winchester, where Rufus was buried in the cathedral. The path Purkis took to Winchester was the origin of the present road called King's Lane. As a reward, Purkis's family was given, in perpetuity, the right to take from the Forest such wood as they could gather 'by hook or by crook, dead bracken and what could be broken but not cut by the axe'. There are many Purkises still in and around the Forest today.

View of Rufus Stone: a site popular with visitors. *[photo by Pier Paolo Strona]*

There has always been much controversy about who killed Rufus: was it Sir Walter, his own brother or another member of the party? What seems probable is that it was murder. Henry I was without doubt the one who most benefited from his brother's death and his subsequent behaviour, including his lack of interest in investigating the death, strongly indicates that, even if he was not the actual murderer, he probably acquiesced in the deed!

Henry seems to have most wisely abstained from further excursions into the Forest. Subsequent kings softened the penalties of Canute's law and hence improved the life of the Foresters. Henry II, in his Charta de Foresta, ruled that "henceforth no man shall lose life or member for taking our deer", although the penalties, as shown by the records, were still heavy on those who took deer from the Forest. Richard I is credited with ending the death and maiming penalties imposed on those taking or attempting to take the King's animals. By this time the Crown was starting to realize the importance of the Forest as a source of timber and firewood as well as pasture (or 'vert' as it is still called). Edward I showed his interest in the vert by making two perambulations in the Forest in an effort to define its limits and stop further encroachments.

Henry VII decided to establish a full-time navy based in Portsmouth and the Solent to replace the Cinque Ports system of requisitioning merchant vessels in time of war. The importance of the Forest as a source of timber immediately began to increase, while its function as a hunting ground started to decline. More trees were planted by Henry VIII, who passed a Statute of Woods in 1543.

The present system of enclosures to protect trees from the animals appears to have been instituted by Elizabeth I, who was well aware of the importance of timber for the construction of her navy. Many of the English ships, including some that fought the Spanish Armada, were constructed with wood from the Forest. Elizabeth was the daughter of Henry VIII and became Queen of England in 1558 on the death of her half sister Mary. Well educated and politically astute, she laid the

Elizabeth 1 (1533-1603)
[National Portrait Gallery, London]

foundations for Britain to become a world power. Elizabeth surrounded herself with able men like Sir William Cecil (Lord Burghley) to govern the country. She supported many sailors in their exploration and conquests, the most prominent being Sir Francis Drake who, by defeating the Armada, gave Britain supremacy on the seas. Her reign is also renowned for many cultural achievements, including poets and writers such as Shakespeare.

Other local industries of strategic importance were saltpetre and charcoal, both used in the manufacturing of gunpowder. Charcoal was also employed in iron smelting and several Forest places names relate to this industry, including Iron Hill Lodge on the opposite side of the road to the entrance to Ashurst Lodge.

From then on, the interest of the Crown in the Forest seems to have declined. James I gave land and trees in the Forest to finance his troops and other expenses and from then on the Forest was seen as an asset to be exploited. Charles I is notorious for having given the Forest as security to his creditors. Charles II gave numerous royal grants of land and timber, particularly to his favourites. He is nevertheless credited with trying to reintroduce wild boar into the Forest, which seem to have disappeared during the 15th century. Another animal that became extinct in the Forest, probably around the 16th century, was the wolf, while the marten seems to have survived until the 19th century.

Although Charles II certainly visited the New Forest – with his lover Nell Gwynn amongst others – during his time the use of the Forest as a royal hunting ground diminished and the office of Keeper became a 'grace and favour' appointment. Charles II gave some woods at Brockenhurst to members of his court, although he also planted new oaks for the future needs of the navy.

By the end of the 17th century, the Forest was in a very bad state and the system of keepers had all but collapsed. Realizing this, William III established the Enclosure Act of 1698 and reforested many acres, but by then the Forest was seriously neglected, inhabited by smugglers, fugitives from justice and other undesirables.

The 17th century saw the appointment of the Lord Warden, who controlled the Forest through a number of Master Keepers. Each of the Masters was in charge of one of the bailiwicks into which the Forest was divided, and each bailiwick in turn was divided into one to three walks with an Underkeeper living in a Lodge. The number of walks proved excessive and eventually some of them disappeared. The Commission of Enquiry of 1677 found, amongst other problems, that

> …the Lodges erected of late years in the Forest are a great means of the
> destruction thereof, not only in the largeness of them in requiring great repairs

Roe deer in the Forest. Photo taken near our Ashurst Lodge. *[photo by Keith Godwin]*

and fuel wood, but in the number of them, also, being nineteen whereas about three score and ten years since there was but three in the whole Forest; and therefore we humbly conceive if they were to be reduced to nine being only so many Bailiwicks or walks it would very much tend to the preservation of the Forest...

The Duke of Bedford was Warden of the Forest from 1746 to 1773 and under his excellent administration many of the excesses of the Forest Keepers and dwellers were curtailed. One of his stewards or deputies was Henry Fielding, author of Tom Jones, who served from 1746 until his death in 1759. Another steward was the notorious Charles Coleman, one of the three stewards or deputies of the duke.

Coleman was characteristic of many of the officers of the Forest at that time and, in a letter to Fielding, was described in these terms: "...there never was so great vermin as C [Coleman] in the Forest"! Corrupt and inefficient keepers were a great problem until the duke took control of the Forest and it took some time for him to remove them from office (including Coleman, who was dismissed in 1750).

Another problem was the population of the Forest itself, most of the inhabitants making a living by pilfering and stealing out of the Forest. A letter from one of the Underkeepers to the duke's agent, Robert Butcher, reads:

I am unhappily situated in and surrounded with a nest of pilfering people...

Even Charles Coleman wrote to the same agent in 1749, complaining:

These places and all the townships back betwixt Lymington and Christchurch, are the most perverse people around the Forest...

Robert Butcher, also received a letter from another of the stewards complaining that:

...I think some of the Keepers have a wrong name, for they are more properly destroyers; and under a very jolly pretence, which they claim as a custom (this is to kill a deer once in six weeks to keep the hounds in blood) they kill more deer and game in a clandestine manner to serve their own private needs, that they kill by warrant.

The dukes' problems were also compounded by the unusual status of the walks under the Duke of Bolton, who refused allegiance to the rest of the Forest. A letter to Robert Butcher dated 1750 from one of his officers states:

Am I [sic] particularly ordered by the Verderers to inform my Lord Duke of Bedford that Mr Dixon (the Duke of Bolton's Underkeep of Burley Walk being much the largest and best walk in the Forest) absolutely refused to make any mention of what bucks he had killed or give account of the said Walk and said he was ordered to do so by his Master.

In spite of the constant opposition, the Duke of Bedford effected major changes in the Forest during his administration, although most of these improvements were later lost.

While the office of Lord Warden originated with the Forest as a hunting ground, the appointment of the Surveyor General of Woods, responsible to the Treasury, was due to the growing interest of the Crown in the timber needed for naval construction. The Surveyor General's position was to become more powerful as the need for timber accelerated and in the 19th century he became the most important officer in the Forest while the office of Lord Warden became increasingly irrelevant and then disappeared.

In 1789 a commission appointed to review the state of the Forest pointed out its parlous state. Every type of excess was committed to exploit the Forest and numerous encroachments were found. Worse was to come in the 19th century, which was the lowest point in the history of the Forest, with keepers indifferent to the numerous encroachments. The custom of setting up a hovel in the Forest

Typical New Forest cottage at the beginning of the 20th Century. Many of these cottages were rapidly built using clay mixed with straw, chopped heather or other local materials, resulting in walls up to 2 feet (0.6m) thick. Many of them are still standing.

to occupy a site dates from this period. Such lodgings were assembled in a single night and a fire kindled so that the Keepers could not eject the new settlers without proper legal process. Because many of the new arrivals were ferocious characters, few Keepers were prepared to argue with them. Gilpin, in his famous book Remarks on Forest Scenery (1794), states:

> …the forest is continually preyed on by the encroachments of inferior people.
> There are multitudes of trespassers, on every side of it, who build their little
> huts, and enclose their gardens, and patches of ground, without leave, or
> ceremony of any kind. The under-keepers, who have constant orders to destroy
> all these enclosures, now and then assert the rights of the forest by throwing
> down a fence; but it requires a legal process to throw down a house, of which
> possession has been taken. The trespasser therefore, as on other wastes, is
> careful to rear his cottage and get into it as quickly as possible. I have known all
> the materials of one of these habitations brought together – the house built –

covered in – the wood removed – a fire kindled – and the family in possession, during the course of a moon-light night.

The situation became so muddled that a Royal Commission was appointed in 1848 to determine the rights of those living in the Forest, and from then on we have amongst other things a clear definition of the Commoners' rights. They are:

RIGHT OF COMMON PASTURE, which is now accessible at all times and used mainly for horses, donkeys and cows. Pasture of sheep is allowed only in cases where it is expressly mentioned.

RIGHT OF MAST during the time of 'pannage' for all hogs and pigs. This is during the acorn season.

RIGHT OF TURBARY upon the open wastes to extract turf for private use. This also includes the right to cut heath and firewood for burning.

RIGHT OF MARL, for the taking away from the open Forest as much marl (a mixture of soil and limestone) as necessary for the improvement of their lands.

RIGHT OF ESTOVER for the cutting of wood. Commoners are entitled to a certain amount of wood per year.

These rights are still with us and as they are vested in the property rather than the owners themselves, they should remain for a long time. The only rights exercised now by some of the Commoners are those of pasture and of mast, the latter particularly declining as the number of working farms in the Forest continues to decrease. The right of pasture, however, is very much used by Commoners with horses and its endurance is ensured by the high proportion of keen horse riders living in the Forest. Many visitors to the Forest do not realize that all the ponies they see roaming freely actually belong to someone.

An important piece of legislation was the Deer Removal Act of 1851. This was an effort to eradicate the original function of the Forest as a royal hunting ground

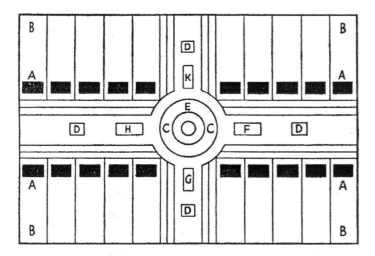

Drawing published in 1722 showing Defoe's plan for settling German refugees from the Palatinate in the New Forest. 7,000 Protestant refugees came to Britain as a result of the religious wars at the time of the Duke of Marlborough. The scheme came to nought while many of the refugees ended up in the American colonies (after Kenchington).

A Farmsteads
B Lands enclosed behind
C Streets and tradesmen's houses
D Wells or conduits
E Church
F Shambles
G Market-house
H Town-hall
K Conduit, stocks, etc.

and replace it by agriculture and forestry. The removal of the deer was at that time welcomed by the Foresters, but the Act also allowed the enclosure of a further 10,000 acres (4,000 ha) of land, to which the Commoners strongly objected. This was followed in 1871 by a Bill for the Disafforestation of the New Forest.

It was through the effort of William Cooper of Broadlands that the Forest was saved. Cooper was an MP who was instrumental in the passing of the 1877 New Forest Act, to which we owe the existence of the Forest. Broadlands (now the residence of the Mountbatten family, who are closely related to the monarchy) was formerly the country house of Lord Palmerston, who appears to have been the father of William Cooper as a result of an affair he had with the wife of Earl Cooper. This may explain Lord Palmerston leaving his estate to William upon his death.

The New Forest Act of 1877 abolished the privileges of the Crown and reinstated in a different format the ancient Court of Verderers, or Swainmate, which had ceased to operate in the 17th century. This body now represented the interests of the Commoners rather than those of the Crown as hitherto. Verderers elected by the Commoners then started fiercely to defend their privileges and rights, and still continue to do so today.

William Cobbett (1763-1835)
[National Portrait Gallery, London]

The period following 1877 also saw the privatization of many properties including lodges, as the 'grace and favour' appointments of Charles II started to lapse.

During the 19th century different schemes were proposed for the Forest, including one by Defoe who suggested that it should be populated with refugees from the Palatinate on the Rhine. One wonders what such an initiative would have meant for the local accent!

World War I saw many changes in the Forest. Numerous camp sites were established and manoeuvres took place over the whole area. A grenade school was set up at Boltons Bench, near Lyndhurst and not far from Ashurst Lodge, and an airfield was built at Beaulieu, which is now used for model aircraft. Another reminder of WWI use of the Forest is the so-called 'Portuguese fireplace' near Lyndhurst, just off the road to Christchurch. This was the cooking area for the Portuguese troops camped in that part of the Forest. A sadder reminder of the war is the graves of soldiers in the churchyard at Brockenhurst. There were also large numbers of trees felled during WWI, and after the war many of them were replaced by fast-growing conifers.

In 1924, as a result of establishing the Civil List, the Office of Woods became the Forestry Commission, which has more autonomy and is separate from the Crown. The Civil List determines payments to the Royal Family after they surrendered to the nation certain rights and properties, including the New Forest.

There were again many changes during World War II, when the Forest became a major military site, with several airfields, two bombing ranges and innumerable encampments, particularly in the run-up to D-Day. It took time and effort to eradicate the effect of all these activities.

The survival of the Forest is mainly due to the poor quality of the soil. But, nevertheless, it is little short of a miracle that there is any Forest left at all after all the encroachments and the further selling of public land that took place at the end of the 19th century.

William Cobbett was an author and politician, renowned for his defence of the poor, and as a critic of social inequality. His views being deemed controversial at the time led him to take refuge in the USA, where he became a journalist until he had to return to England due to his criticism of their government. It was then that he set up in his famous journey through the country, which resulted in his 'Rural Rides' book, a unique record of the state of the countryside at the beginning of the XIX Century. His love of English rural life and concern for the poor set him aside as one of the most influential radical reformers of the period. He remarked of the soil of the Forest at around this time "that a poorer spot than the New Forest there is not in all England, I believe, in the whole world."

He also wrote:

This New Forest is a piece of property as much belonging to the public as the Custom House in London is. There is no man, however poor, who has not a right in it.

In the words of Wise:

Land has higher and nobler offices to perform than to support houses or grow corn – to nourish not so much the body as the mind of man.

THE INHABITANTS

The Forest People

Not all visitors to the Forest have been kind about the inhabitants, who were seen as a race apart, fiercely independent, self-reliant and suspicious of strangers. Gilpin describes them as follows:

> The many advantages, which the borderers on forests enjoy, such as rearing cattle, and hogs, obtaining fuel at an easy rate, and producing little patches of land for the trouble of enclosing it, would add much, one should imagine, to the comfort of their lives. But in fact it is otherwise. These advantages procure them not half the enjoyments of common day-labourers. In general, they are an indolent race; poor and wretched in the extreme. Instead of having the regular returns of a week's labour to subsist on, too many of them depend on the precarious supply of forest pilfer.

One of the writers who best described the natural beauty of the New Forest was William Henry Hudson, a keen naturalist.

Hudson was born in Buenos Aires in 1841, the son of an Irish American family who emigrated from Boston to Argentina. He came to England in 1869 as a result of an illness that had affected his heart and to pursue a better education. He has written excellent books describing the flora and fauna of his two countries, in particular the pampas and Hampshire. His books on Argentina are full of descriptions of its people and customs and it is easy to perceive his deep love for the gauchos of the pampas. Hudson's books on Hampshire concentrate more on the flora and fauna, and when referring to the people, and in particular those in the New Forest, his remarks are unusually critical. In Hampshire Days he wrote:

It must be borne in mind that the Forest area has a considerable population composed of commoners, squatters, private owners, who have inherited or purchased lands originally from the Forest; and of a large number of persons who reside mostly in the villages, and are private residents, publicans, shopkeepers, and lodging house keepers. All these people have an object in common – to get as much as they can out of the Forest.

He appears to forget that, like his beloved gauchos, the Foresters had the ability to live within a different but equally harsh environment. This quality makes him despair:

The New Forest people are, in fact, just what circumstances have made them. Like all organized beings, they are the creatures of, and subject to, the conditions they exist in, and they can not be other than they are – namely parasites of the Forest. And, what is more, they can not be educated, or preached, or worried out of their ingrained parasitical habits and ways of thought. They have had centuries – long centuries – of practice to make them cunning, and the effect of more stronger regulators than those now in use would only be to polish and put a better edge on that weapon which Nature has given them to fight with.

My limited experience of the Forest has nevertheless given me a lot of respect for the self-reliant qualities of its people. They have a dignity of their own as the Forest is a part of England that has been least affected by the feudal system. Foresters are democratic if perhaps a bit too anarchic for Hudson's liking. And as far as cunning is concerned, the gauchos also had plenty of that.

Vesey-Fitzgerald called the Forest inhabitants a "race apart" and said, "There is here in the New Forest a people that has never been conquered – just as the people of Central Wales have never been conquered".

Different theories exist about the origin and composition of the people of the Forest. It is remarkable how many families are still living here since the first records were produced, their names being associated with the Forest since its origins. It is reasonable to expect that some of the physical characteristics of the Celts will be more marked here than in any other part of Hampshire.

Edric Holmes in *Wanderings in Wessex* wrote:

The observant stranger will notice a large proportion of small, dark folk among the inhabitants of the Forest. It is a fascinating matter for conjecture that these may be the remnants of the Iberians that once held South Britain or even, perhaps of a still older people left stranded by the successive races that have swept westwards by way of the uplands to the north.

In addition to these distinctive types, the Forest attracted a large number of gypsies as it provided an ideal environment for their way of life. They made a living out of the Forest by basket-making and broom-making, weaving and other handicrafts. The New Forest gypsies did not mix with the other inhabitants, but nowadays they lead a more settled way of life and some have been absorbed into the mainstream. However, certain surnames are still considered to be 'gypsy' by local people.

Lascelles, who was appointed Deputy Surveyor of the New Forest in 1880, was not fond of the gypsies. In his classic book, Thirty-Five years in the New Forest, he wrote:

The Gypsy population – at some seasons very numerous and often very lawless – almost require a staff to themselves. For many reasons it has not been found practicable to banish them altogether from a Forest that is practically open to all His Majesty's subjects; but there is a code of rules for the regulation of their camps and other proceedings, and a good deal of the time of the keepers is spent enforcing these rules and checking the depredation of these semi-savages.

A Curious Visitor

General Juan Manuel de Rosas, dictator of Argentina between 1829 and 1852. *[Courtesy of Archivo General de la Nación, Buenos Aires]*

Another Argentine exile associated with the Forest is General Juan Manuel Rosas, dictator of the country from 1829 to 1852. In Argentina, General Rosas is seen by many as a great national hero, while his opponents think that he was a blood-thirsty tyrant. Undoubtedly he was a controversial figure. Darwin met Rosas in Patagonia when the latter was fighting the Indians and described him as "a man of extraordinary character with a most predominant influence in the country". His tyrannical rule lasted until 1852 when his army was defeated and he fled to England. He died in exile in 1877 and his body lay buried in Southampton Old Cemetery until recently, mainly because of the passionate debates that erupted every time there was an attempt to repatriate his remains.

Despite being a dictator and having fought a war against Britain, he was well liked and supported by the British community in Buenos Aires. William Hudson recounted how his father was an admirer of the General and that they even had a portrait of Rosas in their house.

When Rosas was deposed, Britain gave him asylum on *HMS Conflict*, a British man-of-war that was then anchored near the port of Buenos Aires. *HMS Conflict* took him to Plymouth, which received him with full military honours, to the dismay of The Times ("Marvellous has been the eagerness of English gentlemen, high in military and naval authority, to grasp his blood-stained hands"). He proceeded to Southampton, where he settled in

Rockstone House in Carlton Crescent until he moved to Burgess Street Farm at Swaythling in 1862.

Rosas tried to run his comparatively small Southampton farm of 400 acres (162 ha) in the same way as he had administered vast Argentine estancias. The results were poor and the business unprofitable. He paid his farm hands well but drove them hard and maintained a close supervision and strict discipline. Rosas remained for ever attached to the customs of his native pampas and was a picturesque figure around town, seated always on good horses in colourful attire. He also enjoyed riding in the Forest, which he described in a letter to one of his supporters in Argentina:

> There exists in this County a completely uninhabited Forest. It measures around
> 10 leagues of longitude and 8 of latitude. It has abundance of deer, hares and
> birds, and all types of animals to hunt. Its grounds, streams, grasses and trees
> are beautiful. There in that unchangeable solitude and uninterrupted silence,
> I find my only distraction as my life is completely private. And because all my
> aspirations are reduced to this type of retirement I have chosen this place where
> this public land is situated.

Little by little his eccentricity became more pronounced and his dislikes more intense. As an arch-conservative, he saw the meeting of the First International in London in 1864 as a calamity. He was against free and compulsory education and thought that trying to educate the lower classes was a mistake. Rosas cultivated the friendship of Lord Palmerston (Foreign Secretary and Prime Minister) whom he made a point of visiting every year in nearby Romsey in what is now the Mountbatten home. He was a fervent admirer of the British monarchy.

In certain ways Rosas was steadfast in his convictions and retained in exile the idea that the best government was an autocratic dictatorship. His constancy made him more and more of an anachronism in a rapidly changing world until he died, mentally unbalanced, in Southampton in 1877. His remains were finally repatriated to Buenos Aires in 1991.

The New Forest ponies are hardy animals, able to sustain themselves with the scarce vegetation of the New Forest. *[photo by Pier Paolo Strona]*

The Ponies

Everybody who visits the Forest for the first time is impressed by the number of ponies that roam freely and apparently wild throughout it. In spite of appearance, these animals all have owners who are Commoners with the right to release them in the Forest.

The New Forest pony has changed its characteristics as a result of crossbreeding, but more recently care has been taken to maintain the breed. Stallions, for instance, cannot be released in the Forest without special approval.

The New Forest pony is an extremely hardy animal, well suited to withstand the rigours of the winter in the open and to feed itself from the sparse vegetation produced by the poor Forest soil.

An attempt to 'improve' the ponies was made by Queen Victoria, who allowed two Arab stallions to cover New Forest mares at New Park, Brockenhurst. The attempt was not successful in terms of numbers but it encouraged others to emulate the experiment. This trend continued until the end of the 19th century, when efforts were made to revitalize the native breed rather than to 'improve' it with animals less well adapted to the conditions prevalent in the Forest.

The Verderers are responsible for looking after the ponies, as well as many other matters. They employ four Agisters, each of whom has responsibility for a district. The tails of the New Forest ponies are cut in four distinctive patterns to prove that their owners have paid their dues and to identify the district to which they belong.

The ponies are rounded up and some selected for sale at various times

View of the corrals at Beaulieu Road where the ponies are gathered for sale. *[photo by Pier Paolo Strona]*

throughout the year at Beaulieu Road. Their fate ranges from becoming riding ponies to being a delicacy at some continental tables.

The Deer

The more striking animals of the Forest are the deer, of which five species are present. The red deer is the biggest and most elegant. They are not seen in many places but they had sometimes visited Ashurst Lodge, where they grazed undisturbed in the evening or early morning.

By far the most common species is the fallow deer, which are certainly

27

Fallow deer herd in the winter.
Another picture taken around our
Lodge. *[photo by Keith Godwin]*

plentiful where I live in Burley. Smaller than the red deer, they move gracefully through the Forest in herds and into gardens to eat roses and other tender plants unless they are well fenced! The deer have become accustomed to our comings and goings as they graze in our paddocks and seem to ignore us yet they never let us get too close. They have distinctive black markings around the tail and usually a pale dappled coat in summer. The fallow deer inhabit the area to the north of the main railway line from Southampton to Bournemouth, while the small Japanese sika deer live south of the line. The sika are very shy. They were brought from Japan during the last century and were released into the Forest from Lord Montagu's Beaulieu estate at the beginning of 1900. There are also a small number of roe deer throughout the Forest; like the sika, they are very timid. The fifth type of deer in the Forest is the muntjac or Chinese variety, which were released from Woburn Park also in around 1900. They are small animals and difficult to see in the Forest and they are few in number.

Lascelles wrote that the original stock was the red deer but that they never grew to be a great herd in the New Forest; the fallow deer instead were and are very numerous. It is believed that they were introduced by the Romans and that they descended from stock from the shores of the Sea of Marmara. In the opinion of Lascelles, the Forest ought to thank the Romans for three very durable imports: "the beech tree, the most beautiful object of the Forest, the fallow deer and the pheasant".

Lascelles was most complimentary about the venison resulting from the New Forest deer and particularly the fallow deer: "I never partook of a deer out of a park that seemed to me to be anything as good as Forest bred in excellence", a comment with which I heartily agree.

As the deer are destructive and damage the vert their number is controlled by regular culling by the Forestry Commission and specially licensed hunters. The 1851 Deer Removal Act was passed in response to the damage they did to the Forest and the consensus was in favour of the Act. As early as 1826, Cobbett complained:

Why, there are more deer bred in Richmond Park alone that would feed all the branches of the Royal family. For what and for whom then are deer kept in the New Forest; and why an expense of hay farms, of sheds, or ricks, or keepers of lodges…

Some Commoners may have been pleased to see most of the deer removed from the Forest within two years of the Act, but the Crown's claim to enclose a further 10,000 acres (4,000 ha) by way of compensation drew vigorous protest. While this conflict continued between Commoners wanting to assert their right to open pasture and the Crown wishing to grow timber, the deer reappeared.

In the words of Hudson:

One can imagine the time come when this one small piece of England which lies between the Avon and Southampton Water will be a sanctuary for all rare and beautiful wildlife and a place of refreshment to body and soul for all men.

MY FAVOURITE PLACES

In what follows I describe the places in the New Forest which, in my opinion, are the more interesting to visit. Their order is irrelevant as I have simply listed them in accordance with a circuit that the visitor to Ashurst Lodge can follow, starting at the nearby village of Lyndhurst.

I have concentrated on buildings and villages, particularly historical ones rather than beautiful landscapes and walks, in part because the latter have been described in innumerable publications. I am aware, however, that this is a personal view of what I consider to be the most interesting places in the Forest and apologize for leaving out many sites that may appeal to other people.

To locate any of them please refer to the map at the end of this book.

Lyndhurst

Lyndhurst is frequently called the 'capital' of the Forest as some administrative offices are located there. It is the nearest town to Ashurst Lodge and its name derives from Old English, meaning 'lime woods'.

Parts of Lyndhurst are still picturesque but the town has been greatly spoilt through being a major road junction. This is ironical as the citizens of Lyndhurst were so much against the railway line from Southampton passing through their woods and town, originally going to only Ringwood, that the station was located outside the town. This is why the station at Ashurst, which is 3 miles (5 km) from the centre of the town was until recently called Lyndhurst Road Station. Visitors to the town arriving by train were ferried from the station by a coach service operated by the owners of the Crown Hotel, who were the proprietors of the garage, both of which still exist in Lyndhurst, although the latter now only sells luxury cars.

This first railway line through the Forest went from Ashurst Station to Ringwood through Brockenhurst, producing a long circular detour around Lyndhurst called 'Castleman's corkscrew', Castleman being a director of the railway, resident in Ringwood and one of the influential citizens who helped to save the woods around Lyndhurst. The section of track from Brockenhurst to Ringwood was dismantled in the 1960s, but the detour resulted in the growth of Brockenhurst, which became a much larger town, particularly after the line was continued to Bournemouth and beyond.

Much has been written about Lyndhurst and not all of it complimentary. W. Hudson wrote:

Lyndhurst is objectionable to me not only because it is a vulgar suburb, a transcript of Chiswick or Plumstead in the New Forest where it is a wrong atmosphere, but also because it is the spot on which London vomits out its annual crowd of collectors, who will its numerous and ever-increasing brand-new red-brick lodging-houses, and who swarm through the adjacent woods and heaths, men, women and children (hateful little pigs!) with their vasculums, beer and treacle pots, green and blue butterfly nets, killing bottles and all the detestable paraphernalia of what they probably called 'nature study'.

Vesey-Fitzgerald wrote, "…and Lyndhurst is a place that one should leave as soon as one can"!

Not everybody feels as negatively as Hudson and Vesey-Fitzgerald about Lyndhurst but I think that it would be greatly improved if a by-pass were built to take the traffic away from the centre of town. Unfortunately, such a move, which

Lyndhurst High Street in the early 1900s. The spire of St Michael and All Angels can be seen in the background. Most of the buildings in the photo are still standing but the road itself has become a busy thoroughfare. *[photo from author's collection]*

requires Parliament's approval, has been defeated time and time again.

The most interesting building in Lyndhurst is the Verderers' Court where that body regularly meet. The name of the court is Swainmote, which derives from the name 'Swain' given to the Freeholders of the Forest. It deals nowadays with all sorts of Forest rights and customs, including rights of way. The Verderers' Court is a fine building called the King's (or Queen's) House, dating mainly from 1634, although the Verderers' Hall itself was built in 1388. 'Rufus's stirrup' hangs over the fireplace in the Hall. The stirrup is supposed to have been to test whether a dog could be allowed to run free in the Forest. Those animals that were too large to pass through the stirrup were liable to have "three claws of the forefoot cut off by the skin."

The presence of the King's House ensured that Lyndhurst had its share of royal visitors. Edward I spent time at Lyndhurst between 1278 and 1289 and his Queen, Eleanor of Castile, lived there most of the time during his campaign against the Welsh. It is believed that Charles II visited the town frequently while New Park was being renovated as his hunting lodge.

George III paid two visits to the Forest and during the first of them in 1789 he resided in his Lyndhurst house, then occupied by the Warden, the Duke of Gloucester. Madame D'Arblay, a witness to the visit, gives us an insight into a different era when she recorded in her diary:

> During the King's dinner, which was in a parlour looking into the garden, he permitted the people to come to the window, and their delight and rapture, in seeing their monarch at table, with the evident hungry feeling it occasioned, made a contrast of admonition and deprivation truly comic [sic]. They crowded, however, so excessively, that this can not be permitted them no more. They broke down all the paling, and much of the edges and some of the windows, and all by eagerness and multitude, for they were perfectly civil and well-behaved.

Another interesting building in Lyndhurst is the parish church of St Michael and

All Angels, which is situated on high ground to the west. Although the present church was built in 1863, there has been a church on the site since time immemorial. The previous one was built by George III and was popular due to its royal patronage. There are many interesting details about this church and it is worth a visit. The main artistic decoration is a fresco of *The Parable of the Wise and Foolish Virgins* by Lord Leighton. Two of the windows are the work of the Pre-Raphaelite Edward Burne Jones. It is the burial place of Alice Hargreaves, daughter of the Dean of Christ Church College, Oxford. As a girl, she inspired Charles Lutwidge Dodgson, mathematics don at the college and better known as Lewis Carroll, to write *Alice in Wonderland*. The Church provides an imposing presence in Lyndhurst with its 50-metre spire of red and yellow bricks.

View of the Altar at Saint Michael and All Angels, with Lord Leighton's fresco of the Wise and Foolish Virgins in the background. *[photo by Pier Paolo Strona]*

Old photograph showing the green in the centre of Minstead in the early 1900s. The pub in the background is the Trusty Servant, famous for its old sign at the entrance, a copy of the one in Winchester College. *[photo from the author's collection]*

Minstead

Minstead is one of the most charming villages in the Forest and can be easily reached going north from Lyndhurst along the main road towards Cadnam and turning left after a mile and a half.

Minstead has what can be described as a typical New Forest green. Across the green is a pub with an unusual sign, The Trusty Servant, which is the same as that hanging in Winchester College. It is said that a passing painter sold the sign to the pub owner, who changed the name of the house accordingly. The verse accompanying the picture is as follows:

A Trusty Servant's portrait would you see,
This emblematic figure well survey,
The Porker's Servant not nice in diet shows,
The Padlock Shut no secret he'll disclose.

Patient the Ass his master's wrath will bear,
Stiffness in errand the Stagg's feet declare
Loaded his Left Hand apt to labour saith
The Vest his neatness Open hard his faith,
Girt with his Sword his Shield upon his arm,
Himself and his Master he'll protect from harm.

This 16th-century poem and the corresponding picture hang outside the kitchen at Winchester College, presumably from the days when the pupils had personal servants.

From the green, a road leads to the church, which is set at the top of a little hill and deserves a visit.

Vesey-Fitzgerald describes Minstead church in the following words:
Architecturally it is a positively astonishing jumble of styles. Originally it was
Norman (it was first mentioned in 1272) and it has a truly remarkable Norman
font. The chancel is Gothic but built in some part with rounded Norman

The "jumble of styles" Church at Minstead. *[photo from the author's collection]*

View of the curious three-decker pulpit at Minstead Church. *[photo by Pier Paolo Strona]*

stones. The north doorway is transitional. The porch is seventeenth century, the tower eighteenth. There is a south transept of about the year 1800 and the remains of a fifteenth century chancel screen. And there is the great three-decker pulpit. The whole might so easily be horrible – and blends perfectly. And then there are the family pews of Castle Malwood and Minstead Lodge. These pews are enormous, more like rooms than pews, for they have fireplaces and are backed by large windows.

This description of Minstead Church is still accurate, with the exception that the font is now believed to be Saxon rather than Norman because of its primitive carving. The font was dug up in the garden of the rectory in 1893, presumably having been buried there to protect it from the zeal of Cromwell's soldiers who disfigured many of the mainly Royalist New Forest parish churches.

The churchyard is worth a visit. In it lies Sir Arthur Conan Doyle, the creator of Sherlock Holmes, next to his wife under a large oak. Although he died in Sussex he had a cottage in the Forest in his last years, during which he became deeply involved in spiritualism. The cottage is on the River Cadnam not far from Minstead and is called Bignell Wood. Conan Doyle was first buried in Sussex but his body was transferred to Minstead churchyard when his family decided to settle in the Forest cottage.

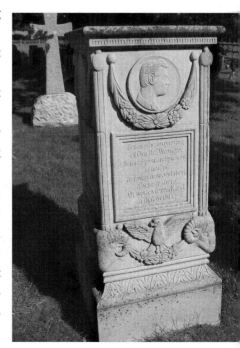

Right: Tombstone of Christopher Tower (1915-1998), diplomat and Orientalist and a lover of Greece. Upon his death, he endowed his old Christchurch College in Oxford with a Poetry studentship, although his own poems were terrible. One of them of mystical character is engraved on the side of the plinth. It reads:

Before the imparting of our 'Be'! We were
Before a 'past and present', 'is not' 'is';
Before a 'now and then' or 'here' or 'there'
Or we'd externalised a 'that others'.

38

Another interesting character buried in this graveyard is Christopher Tower (1915–1998), a diplomat and poet who became an expert in Arab affairs and Chief Adviser to the King of Libya. His books were not successful but his love of poetry led him to endow his old Oxford college with a fund to encourage aspiring poets.

Another site of interest to the north of Minstead is Castle Malwood, which is an old fort, in the middle of which is situated Malwood Lodge, where Rufus is alleged to have stayed the night before his death. It now belongs to Southern Electricity and is not accessible to the public.

North of Minstead also lies the Rufus Stone which is the place where the king was supposed to have been slain. The inscription on two sides of the monument reads as follows:

Here stood the oak tree on which an arrow shot by Sir Walter Tyrrell at a stag glanced and struck King William II surnamed Rufus on the breast of which he

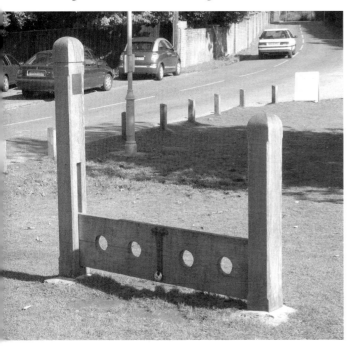

Centre: Stocks in Minstead Village Green. They were used from the Middle Ages to early 1900s to punish small acts of misbehaviour. The ones in the photograph held peoples ankles and exposed them to the contempt of their fellow villagers. *[photo from the author's collection]*

Curious gravestone in Minstead Churchyard dedicated to the memory of Mr Thomas White who died in 1842. Notice the cut-out space preceding the word 'husband'. The word 'faithful' was engraved there, but his widow decided to remove it when she was made aware of his real behaviour! *[photo from the author's collection]*

instantly died on August 2nd 1100.

King William II surnamed Rufus being slain as before related was laid on a cart belonging to one Purkiss and drawn from hence to Winchester and buried in the Cathedral church of that city.

While it is doubtful that this is the actual spot where Rufus was killed, the family names Tyrrell and Purkis persist in the New Forest.

Fritham

The northern part of the New Forest is much less populated than the rest, with more open spaces and flat lands that give the area the appearance of a wilderness. Fritham is the most interesting settlement in this area and, in the words of Wise (1862):

Fritham is thoroughly in the forest; and few spots can equal it in interest…close round it lie the barrows of the Kelt, and the potteries of the Roman, covering acres of ground with the banks which mark the site of the workmen's houses.

Wise was referring to the cottages located in the valley below, which were built to accommodate those working at the then prosperous gunpowder mill, which was an important source of employment for the region. Before that time, Fritham was notorious for being a smugglers' village, located along the route taken by the contraband convoys coming from the coast around Lymington and passing through Burley. This activity reached its climax in the 1700s when import duties were very high.

Fritham was better known for its association with gunpowder and in particular with the Schultze Company, which took over from an earlier enterprise. The first gunpowder company was established in 1861 and consisted of a series of buildings located around Eyeworth Lodge, set in a very beautiful spot in the Forest. The Lodge was leased to the company in 1855 as one of the

The Schultze factory reservoir in Eyeworth nowadays. Its construction was bitterly opposed at the time, but it is now a tourist attraction. *[photo from the author's collection]*

sales that took place following the Deer Removal Act of 1851. The neighbouring factory buildings were constructed in 1859. Production of traditional gunpowder started in 1861 with not much success because the explosive has the disadvantage of producing a substantial amount of smoke and giving a powerful recoil. The factory went out of business in 1869.

The facilities of the failed enterprise were taken over by the Schultze Company, which had obtained a licence to manufacture smokeless gunpowder, originally based on the treatment of cotton using nitric acid, a German invention. Captain Schultze, a Prussian artillery officer, perfected the process by using wood pulp instead of cotton.

The company developed the site further and built a reservoir because the

Photograph showing the staff of Schultze's Gunpowder Works in Fritham. The village was then a busy and prosperous place. *[photo from the author's collection]*

process required large quantities of water. The construction of the reservoir was originally bitterly opposed by the Commoners but it now remains as a recreational area.

The Schultze Company did not prosper until the appointment of a gifted self-taught chemist, R.W.S. Griffith, who joined the company in 1874 and steered it towards success. He died in 1906 after 32 years of association with Fritham and the factory.

The turning point for the company came in 1878 when the samples of Schultze's powder were successfully tried in a series of trials arranged by The Field Magazine. From then on, in the words of an 1895 brochure:

> …the prosperity of the company has been increasing year by year and the sale
> of the powder has gone up so rapidly and so continuously that the factory has
> had to be constantly enlarged to cope with the ever increasing demand for
> Schultz's [sic] gunpowder.

The Schultze Gunpowder Company changed Fritham into a village with a population in excess of 200 by 1904 until the company eventually moved to Redbridge in Southampton, a better location for transportation of the products. As a consequence, the mills in Fritham were shut down in 1911.

Burley

John Wise stated in his famous book *The New Forest*: "Burley itself, is one of the most primitive of Forest hamlets, the village suddenly losing itself amongst the holms and hollies, and then reforming itself again in some open space." Although modern Burley cannot be considered primitive, there is a certain wildness about it in spite of its considerable growth in recent years. It was, after all, a meeting

Burley, "one of the most primitive Forest hamlets", according to Wise. *[photo from the author's collection]*

place of smugglers and other fugitives at one time in the Forest. John Wise wrote:

> In the New Forest itself, till within the last thirty years, smuggling was a recognized calling. Lawlessness was the rule during the last century. Warners says that he had then seen twenty or thirty wagons laden with logs, guarded by two or three hundred horsemen, each bearing two or three 'tubs', coming over Hengistbury Head, making their way, in the open day, past Christchurch to the Forest. At Lymington, a troop of bandits took possession of the well-known Ambrose Cave, on the borders of the Forest, and carried on, not only smuggling but wholesale burglary. The whole county was plundered. The soldiers were at last called out, the men tracked, and the cave entered. Booty to an enormous extent was found. The Captain turned King's evidence, and confessed that he had murdered upwards of thirty people, whose bodies had been thrown down a well, where they were found.

The history of the village has been reported in great detail in an excellent book by Félicité Hardcastle. The original village seems to have started with the manor

The village of Ringwood as it was in the 1900s. Ringwood was historically part of the Forest, although it is now just outside its official boundary. The village dates from Saxon times and has been, and still is, a traditional market town of the New Forest with a Charter dating back to 1226. *[photo from the author's collection]*

house and Burley is the name of the family who held the office of bailiff in the 13th century. There were at that time nine bailiwicks in the Forest, of which Burley was by far the largest and was divided into two 'walks', those of Burley and Holmsley.

The land appears to have been reported in the Domesday Book (1086) as part of Rinceveda (modern Ringwood), which was a Royal Manor. The name of the village itself is variously recorded as Burgelea (1178), Burlegh (1212) and Burghley (1301). Richard Coates put forward an interpretation that the name may have meant the wood (lea) of the town (burh) of Ringwood. According to Kenchington, Burley's entry in the Domesday Book is registered under the name Achelet (Oakley) and is recorded as two tenements comprising the modern equivalent of 400 to 640 acres of cleared land.

The first recorded lord of the manor of Burley was Roger, who held 120 acres (49 ha) in 1212, and he was followed by Robert de Burley, under whom the property continued to prosper. It was Richard of Burley who built the first manor house, some time before 1250. The same Richard was convicted for encroaching on the king's land but granted a pardon by the king himself. Later on, the manor was under Sir Simon de Burley, who appears to have been a distant relative of the original family as they did not produce any male heirs in the direct family line. Simon de Burley (1336–1388) was an accomplished scholar who served in the fleet fighting against the Spanish pirates and was also lord of the manor in a place called Beurley in Aquitaine, where he owned vineyards. The Black Prince appointed him tutor to his son Richard and as Constable of the Cinque Ports. Unfortunately, his promising career was cut short after he was charged with treason and executed in the Tower in 1388, in spite of the pleas of the king.

It is difficult to know what happened to the lordship of the manor after that but, as was usual in these cases, the land must have reverted to the Crown.

In 1551 the manor was divided and John Batten was appointed lord. The land stayed in the hands of the Batten family until 1723. The Bailiwick of Burley, as distinct from the Lordship, was held by the Earl of Pembroke by grant of

Elizabeth I in 1570. At around 1609 it became the responsibility of the Earl of Southampton.

Towards the end of the 17th century, the Bailiwick of Burley was in the hands of the Dukes of Bolton, who as Keepers controlled the area as their own private kingdom. In the words of Lascelles, the Duke of Bolton

> for nearly 130 years exercised a sort of imperium in the Forest difficult to understand or explain … During all these years the Dukes of Bolton controlled, as it were, a forest of their own, within the limit of the bailiwick. They seemed to have exercised all forestall rights … exactly as if that part of the Forest belonged to them. And it is perhaps from that cause that Burley, in its old form, before it became a city of villas, was ever intolerant of anything like Forest law and custom, and always prone to contention.

The land grant to the dukes ended in 1786 but was extended for a further period. Eventually in 1809 the Crown – for reasons that are not clear – purchased the interest in the grant for a considerable sum.

After passing through various hands, the manor became the property of Colonel John Carnac, who held it for only four years (1776–1780). This gentleman is most probably the same General John Carnac (1716–1800) who fought with Clive of India and was behind the scheme to develop the Polygon in Southampton. He was described as an "aggressive and confident officer".

In 1780 James Mowbray purchased the property and pulled down the original house, building in its place another, laying out a park with a lake and planting the trees, many of which are still there. James left the property to his sisters and they relied on their steward, Thomas Eyre, a colourful local character, and on the executor of their father's will, a Mr Charles Shaw Lefevre. The Lefevres were a family of French Huguenots originally from Rouen, who were obliged to leave France in 1680 as a consequence of the Edict of Nantes. Charles became lord of the manor and when he died in 1823, the property passed to his wife who in turn left it to the second of her three sons, Sir John Shaw Lefevre. The eldest of the

brothers became a Member of Parliament for Hampshire, and rose to be Speaker of the House of Commons. Upon his retirement he was created Viscount of Eversley, this being the name of woods north of Burley. The second son and lord of the manor of Burley attended Cambridge and had a distinguished academic career. Of special interest to us is that he was one of the co-founders of the University of London and acted as its Vice-Chancellor for 20 years. He was a renowned scholar of mathematics and literature and was reported to be able to converse in all European languages!

In 1834 the manor house became the property of George Rooke Farnoll, who,

Burley Manor built in 1780 and renovated in the 1850s in the then fashionable Elizabethan style. It is now an hotel with equestrian facilities. *[photo by Pier Paolo Strona]*

after losing a court case against the local vicar, decided to move on. Colonel W.C.D. Esdaile brought the house in 1852 but rebuilt it in the pseudo-Elizabethan style so popular at the time. This is basically the house that is still standing. When Colonel Esdaile died, the manor was left in trust to his niece and finally sold after her death and the expiration of the lease. After extension and alterations, the manor was converted into the Burley Manor Hotel in 1933.

In addition to the manor house now converted into a hotel, the village has a few other interesting sites.

The church itself, although appearing older, dates from 1839 and was built on land donated by the Lefevre family. The Queen's Head pub is most probably the oldest house in Burley and its connections with the smuggling trade were confirmed by the discovery in recent years of a cellar containing pistols, old coins and bottles.

Another place of interest in Burley is the shop called A Coven of Witches. It was opened by Sybil Leek, who in the 1950s was the village witch and she started a coven in the Forest, which I believe, is still active today. She used to wear a long black coat and carry a crow on her shoulder and was versed in the ways of the Forest and the gypsies. She decided to emigrate to California, where she became a well-known witch and wrote several books on witchcraft. A picture of her is displayed in the fireplace of her old shop.

Sybil Leek has been described as "the world's most celebrated witch" of her time. She claimed descent from a family of witches on her maternal side and from an early age knew that she possessed special powers. Her ancestors could be traced back to southern Ireland and included the famous witch Molly Leigh, who died in 1663 and is buried just on the edge of St John's Church graveyard in Burslem, Staffordshire. Sybil's father was a gentle scholar to whom she owed most of her education. He was by trade a civil engineer with roots in Imperial Russia.

At an early age she was initiated as a high priestess in a coven in France and shortly after moved with her family to the New Forest. She wrote:

The Coven of Witches Shop of Sybil Leek, the Burley Village Witch. *[photo from the author's collection]*

In Lyndhurst, the Queen Town of the New Forest, I became friendly with the Romanies, the wandering tribes who lived by their own laws and despised the "gorgios" (people of non-gypsy origin)…It did not take me long to see that with these gypsy tribes the elements of the Old Religion still survived.

Sybil lived with the gypsies for about a year during which she learnt how they use witchcraft and the secrets of the Forest. They knew about the properties and powers of herbs and the ways of the animals of the Forest.

The gypsies did not take part in the organized Sabbats held in the New Forest by the four covens that have been in existence since William Rufus was killed. When the religious days came along the gypsies would leave me alone and I would go to join the Horsa Coven which met on the outskirts of Burley. *[Sybil was the High Priestess of the Horsa Coven. Horsa means 'the sign of the Horse' in the New Forest.]*

She explained:

> The New Forest covens always have their full complement of thirteen people in each group: equal number of male and female plus the High Priestess.

After leaving the gypsies, she returned to the family home and opened her shop in Burley. She recounts that she was forced to leave her beloved New Forest because the landlord refused to renew the lease if she did not publicly denounce witchcraft.

Regarding the character of witches, she explained:

> Magic is a joyous exceptional experience which leads to a sense of well-being, and there is nothing we witches love more. So we strive to bring this about…by the use of our particular religion, by keeping close to nature, by seeking harmony in ourselves and our environment…

She seems to have enjoyed America and in particular wrote in very complimentary terms about Boston, a place also dear to us, where our Institute has its US office:

> It was in Boston that I first discovered something of the magic of America. In Boston the gulf between America and the New Forest was lessened.

Burley Hill

My home is called Burley Hill and is situated between Burley and Burley Street. It originally had a plot of approximately 100 acres (40 ha) of which 50 or so still remain attached to the house, which is situated at the top of the hill.

According to Hardcastle in *Records of Burley*, some of the lands belonging to Burley Hill were called Burconibus or Assart lands, which were royal gifts. ('Assart' is a word of Norman origin meaning to root up the trees and break the ground for cultivation.)

The view from Burley Hill is now obscured by dense woods but it was different in Gilpin's time. He describes the view then:

> After we leave these dreary pales, the country, here and there, breaks out towards Holmsly Lodge; but nothing is very interesting till we arrive at the brow of Burley Hill. From this height we survey a grand sweep of different reserves of woody distance, spreading around a semicircular plain of several miles in extent; known by the name of Mark-vey bottom.
>
> Every species of country, cultivated, as well as uncultivated, when melted down into distance, has a fine effect; as we have often observed; but the forest-distance is among the richest – such as the general view from Burley Hill, continuously varying its appearance as we descend.

When the Burley Manor Estate was broken up and sold in 1894 by Colonel Esdaile, the whole of Burley Hill was bought (for £3,698 and 3d) by Blanche Mary Shore Clough, widow of the poet Arthur Hugh Clough (1819–1861). In the following year the first house was built for Mrs Clough and her daughter, Blanche Athena, and this is now my home. The architect, well known at that time, was James Ransome (1865–1944), who had been consulting architect to the Government of India where he was responsible for some interesting buildings, including Wellesley Place in Calcutta and Government House in Chittagong (now in Bangladesh). In 1896 Blanche's son – born in 1859 and also named

Castle Hill encampment near Burley Street. It comprises an area of around 5 acres (2 Ha) and the ramparts rise 13ft (4m) above the bottom of the ditch, which can still be clearly seen in many parts. The ground slopes very rapidly towards the West with the encampment at the top of the hill commanding a view of the whole valley (after Williams-Freeman).

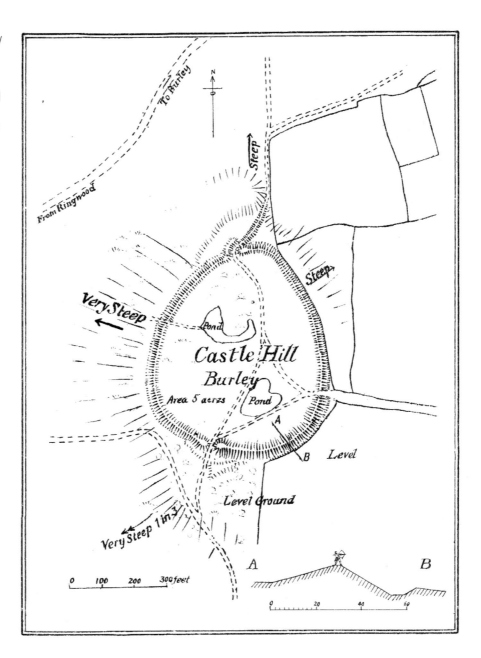

Arthur H. Clough – built a house, very different in style, for himself and his wife, Eleanor (née Freshfield), on the adjacent Castle Hill.

He then went on to develop and build around Burley Hill and elsewhere, and it is after this member of the Clough family that the roads in Burley and Ringwood are named. They were an interesting family both for their achievements and for their connections.

Although little read nowadays, Clough's poems are still in print and were frequently on the syllabus at schools and universities until a generation ago. He was a star pupil at Rugby and a lifelong friend of Matthew Arnold, man of letters and son of the famous Headmaster at Rugby. Clough was appointed Warden at University College London by 1850; he moved in literary and academic circles, held radical views and was driven by a strong sense of duty and service. Through his wife, Blanche Mary Shore, whom he married in 1854, he met many leading political figures of the day and was drawn into Florence Nightingale's web. She made him secretary of the Nightingale Fund after the Crimean War and he became her general factotum for a while.

The Shore family was wealthy and well connected. They tended to be Unitarians, radical freethinkers and reformers, and included among their members successful entrepreneurs and politicians. Blanche Mary was cousin – twice over – to Florence Nightingale whose father was, in fact, a Shore who had changed his name in order to inherit from a wealthy, but childless, uncle. Clough's wife and her children lived for many years in the Nightingale household at Embley Park near Romsey. Florence had Cabinet ministers at her beck and call, both there and in London, and was surrounded by admirers. However, she was demanding and Clough, whose health had never been robust, became exhausted. Apparently Blanche Mary urged him to go abroad to escape and recover his health, which he did, but he died, aged 42 (ironically in Florence) shortly after his daughter, Blanche Athena, was born. He named her but never saw her.

Blanche Athena's brother, Arthur, studied Classics and Moral Science at

View of Burley Hill House from the garden, described in 1945 as "a charming Queen Anne residential property of moderate size".

Trinity College, Cambridge, and was awarded a First. This was not an option for his sister (always known as 'Thena') because, although her mother was progressive and she received a good education, women were not admitted to Cambridge University. Her father's sister, Anne Jemina Clough, had devoted her life to the cause of women's education and was a founder member of the Association for Promoting the Higher Education of Women in Cambridge, and, of course, an inspiration to Thena. She joined her aunt there as a student in 1884 when the right of women to attend lectures had finally been won, though they could not be allowed to sit exams to be awarded degrees until much later.

Her aunt was the first Principal of Newnham College, which had started out as a small hostel but had a new hall of residence in 1875. In 1888 Thena became her assistant and secretary and was herself made Principal later. When she retired in 1923, women were at last awarded 'titular' degrees but were still not permitted to be full members of the university.

Thena loved the New Forest. She knew it well from the time the family lived in the Nightingale household at Embley Park but Burley Hill House was not built until 1895. Burley Hill House became hers following her mother's death in 1905. Her brother and his wife continued living on the adjacent hill at Castletop. He employed many people locally, normally in construction but also in agriculture.

Thena brought many friends to Burley Hill. While some were supporters of the fight for women's suffrage, others had connections to the Bloomsbury Group – certainly Lytton Strachey, the author of Eminent Victorians, and his sisters were house guests – but most were from Cambridge and actively involved in the long struggle for men and women to be treated equally there and for Newnham College to prosper. "There were times during long vacations when the entire business of Newnham appears to have been conducted from Burley Hill," according to Gillian Sutherland in her book *Faith, duty, and the power of mind: The Cloughs and their circle 1820-1960*.

Neither Anne Jemima nor Blanche Athena married or had children. Blanche died in 1960, at which time she was living at Hyde near Fordingbridge; she was almost 99. Women were not awarded full degrees at Cambridge until 1948.

After her mother's death in 1905, Burley Hill House passed to Blanche Athena. Her brother continued living in Castle Top and built houses locally and further afield. He and his wife are remembered for their charity to foreign refugees during the First World War. Blanche Athena Clough gifted the land and building for the Village Parish Hall on December 31st, 1907.

Blanche had never separated her affairs from her brother's so that when he was rendered bankrupt after the Wall Street crash, her house was sold to Sir Cecil Lyndsay Budd, KBE. Sir Cecil was a businessman, chairman of the British Metal Exchange, and he and his family lived at Burley Hill House until 1945, when the property was offered at auction. It was then described in the brochure as "a charming Queen Anne residential property of a moderate size standing about 300 ft [90 m] above sea level, amidst wooded surroundings, facing south with

Florence Nightingale (1820-1910) She is universally acknowledged as the founder of modern nursing. Attracted to nursing from an early age, her chance to put her principles into practice came during the Crimean War, when she took charge of the Scutari Hospital in the Bosforos. Her care for the British soldiers made her a heroine. Following this, she set up the Nursing School at St. Thomas' Hospital in London, which became a model for all the others. Although born in Florence, Italy, she spent the early part of her life in the New Forest area and was buried in the churchyard of East Wellow Village. [National Portrait Gallery, London]

extensive views." It consisted of four reception rooms, ten bedrooms and three bathrooms; the whole area covered 87 acres (35 ha) and included eight cottages. It makes you think what "moderate" meant in 1945! The extensive views over the Solent and the Isle of Wight are difficult to imagine but the trees in the surrounding woods may not have been as high as they are now. By this time, various building plots had been sold off.

The auction took place in November 1945 and the property was sold to a Major John Mann-Thomson of the Cavalry Club, Piccadilly, by deed of December 21st, 1945 for the sum of £19,000. He seems to have lived here only briefly and sold the house to Brigadier Sidney Gerald Howes of Forest Corner, near Ringwood. I am not sure what happened then, but the house was offered for sale again at an auction in Burley Manor Hotel on April 20th, 1955. It is not clear if a sale took place at the auction, but on October 11th, 1955 the house became the property of Commander John Rose Westmacott for the sum of £9,000, the frequent changes and drop in price indicating that the house was falling on bad times.

The Westmacott family continued to sell parts of the estate at different times until the sons (to whom the house had been transferred in 1972) sold the property to a Saudi Arabian royal Prince, Ahmed Bin Saud bin Abdul Aziz, in 1983. Prince Ahmed extended Burley Hill, adding a new floor to the west wing and a covered swimming pool and games room, in addition to making many other improvements to the grounds and gardens. The house was also lavishly decorated and carpeted, making it a most attractive residence. The Prince was popular in the village and surrounding area for his generosity and friendliness. On June 10th, 1993 my wife and I bought the property and since then we have extended the house further.

Rhinefield House

Sometimes we take our guests and visitors to Rhinefield House, which is situated in the middle of the Forest and provides an ideal setting for conferences and banquets.

The name Rhinefield is misleading in relation to the European river and is variously given in documents from the 14th century as Ryefield or Riefelde. Richard Coates speculates that it may derive from Rygefeld, which is Old English meaning 'rye open land'. A 15th-century form of the name appears to have been Rynefeld.

Rhinefield was one of the residences of the Master Keeper, and a record exists that in 1628 the Earl of Holland spent some money for work on what was then called Great Rynefield Lodge.

Rhinefield House – view from the Gardens. 100 year old new Elizabethan style. *[photo from the author's collection]*

As the use of the Forest as a royal hunting ground died out, by 1859 Rhinefield became the residence of the Forest nurseryman, who created an ornamental drive and planted numerous trees in the grounds.

At the end of the 19th century there was a move to privatize the Forest (how history repeats itself!) and many of the lodges were sold. Rhinefield was bought by the Walker family, who owned the Eastwood Colliery, near Nottingham (incidentally, of D.H. Lawrence fame). The only daughter of the family became engaged to Royal Navy Lieutenant Munro and was given £250,000 to build a house in the grounds of Rhinefield. The couple married in 1887 and adopted the name Walker-Munro. They then started building the house and other ancillary buildings.

The great house itself has the aspect of a neo-Gothic castle and consists of a series of large reception rooms, the apartments of Mr and Mrs Walker-Munro and four suites for the four daughters she believed she would have. Unfortunately, the only child of that marriage was a son, Ian, born in 1889, of whom she took scant notice. He joined the army, fighting in France during World War I and, after becoming a major, emigrated to Kenya where his father helped him to become a farmer. He married in 1919 and had four sons.

Mrs Walker-Munro was not pleased with her son and planned to disinherit him, leaving her fortune to charity, but she died in 1934 before she had time to sign the appropriate will. This left Rhinefield in the hands of her son until his death in 1950 when it was sold.

Several different enterprises were accommodated there without much success until, in 1972, an entrepreneur bought the property. He restored some of the grounds, which were in very poor shape and improved the house. During this period the house was used for functions including the then popular medieval banquets. In 1982 the house was acquired by a company that developed Rhinefield into a hotel with conference facilities and timeshare apartments.

The most impressive room in the house is the great hall with a hammer-beam roof resembling the one in Westminster Hall. The hall incorporates a large

The Church of St Saviour's in Brockenhurst, built by the Walker-Munro family. *[photo by Pier Paolo Strona]*

fireplace, which bears the date 1653 and is the only reminder of the previous Keeper's Lodge. In keeping with the variety of styles in the house, the dining room is beautifully panelled with a large carving on the mantelpiece representing the defeat of the Spanish Armada. Other smaller rooms are decorated in Italian and French styles, the most surprising being the Alhambra room. This is a smoking room given as a Christmas present by Mrs Walker-Munro to her husband upon his return from abroad. The room was inspired by the Alhambra Palace and the walls have the type of gesso work one associates with Mudejar architecture. Below this the walls are covered in beautiful Moorish tiles. The inscriptions in the plaster are in Arabic characters proclaiming "There is no God but Allah and Mohammed is his Prophet" among other things. A mosaic floor and onyx column adds to the lightness of the room. The bronze lantern is inscribed with verses from the *Rubáiyát of Omar Khayyám*, while on the dome itself Stars of David made with Venetian glass can be seen. The feeling when sitting there has been likened to being shut inside a jewel case.

It is interesting that the house had, as early as a century ago, an air-conditioning system for cold and hot air working with a gas engine using the coal brought from Mrs Walker-Munro's mines.

Several stories are still told about the lady of the house, who appears to have had a very strong character. Relationships with the locals were sometimes strained. The Walker-Munro family, for instance, styled themselves 'Lord of the Manor at Rhinefield', which brought them into conflict with a local family, the Morants, who were 'Lord of the Manor of Brockenhurst and Rhinefield.' Their relationship became so strained that the Walker-Munros refused to attend the same church as the Morants and in 1903 decided to build their own, now St Saviour's in Brockenhurst. Once again, things did not work out as planned because Mrs Walker-Munro had an argument with their own vicar – who was also a relative – and decided to stop work on the new church. Because of this the church was not licensed as a burial ground on the death of her husband in 1923 and she decided, rather than letting him lie beside the hated Morants, to inter him in a copse on their home farm, Oberfarm, until the church was completed.

Brockenhurst

Brockenhurst is situated between Lyndhurst and Lymington. It is an old Saxon village mentioned in the Domesday Book but it grew into a town in 1847 with the arrival of the railway.

Carey's Manor, now a hotel, was built at the end of the 19th century on the site of an early building of John Carey, who was a Forester at the time of Charles II. Another house, called Brockenhurst Park, belonging to the local squire – a member of the Morant family – was destroyed by fire in recent times. Members of this family, which bought the whole of the parish in the 18th century, were the lords of the manor and are still connected with Brockenhurst.

Brockenhurst has two churches; the older relatively far from the village, is called St Nicholas'. It has been described by Vesey-Fitzgerald as follows:

> The Old Church, which is built upon an artificial mound at the top of a little
> hill, has a Norman doorway on the south side, a chancel arch of very early and

plain Norman work, and a square font of Purbeck marble which must be very nearly as old as the chancel arch.

The graveyard has the names of many soldiers, especially from New Zealand, who died, in a large temporary hospital, consisting of many huts, which was built in Brockenhurst during World War I. In a separate enclosure there are a series of graves of the Morant family. It also has the grave of the snake-catcher, a local character known as 'Brusher' Mills, who sold his catch to London Zoo and

The old St Nicholas Church in Brockenhurst. *[photo by Pier Paolo Strona]*

The grave of 'Brusher Mills' at Brockenhurst Church Cemetery. In the background, the monument to the New Zealanders who died in Brockenhurst Hospital during the First World War. [photo by Pier Paolo Strona]

right: Early New Forest post card showing Brusher Mills next to the hut in which he lived. [photo from the author's collection]

prepared oils and remedies derived from the reptiles. Brusher Mills was a popular character around Brockenhurst in spite of his hermit-like existence in the woods and his habit of consuming a whole bottle of rum every evening!

Brusher's dwelling was a simple hut similar to those set up by the charcoal-burners, who until recently continued to practise their prehistoric trade in the Forest. Their product was valuable in the manufacture of Roman and other pottery for which the Forest was well known, and was also used in the preparation of gunpowder and the melting of metals. Charcoal-burning disappeared from the Forest after World War II.

The second church in Brockenhurst, St Saviour's, built by the Walker-Munro family, is situated near the centre of the village in the opposite direction from St Nicholas'.

New Park

Leaving Brockenhurst for Lyndhurst along the A337 we find New Park, now a hotel, on the left. It was one of the original hunting lodges of the Forest and some of the beams in the present building are said to be 12th century. During the Restoration, Charles II made the house his preferred Forest Lodge and the present building was renovated at that time (1670). He was a shrewd politician as well as a tolerant man, partial to the ladies. Attracted by the sciences, he also promoted the development of the Navy which, combined with his fondness for history, attracted him to the New Forest. The oldest doors in the hotel still have their handles in the shape of acorns in remembrance of Charles II, who once escaped his pursuers by hiding in the trunk of a dead oak tree. He visited New Park frequently, sometimes with Nell Gwynn,

Charles II (1630-1685)
He became King in 1660 following the restoration of the Monarchy and after his father Charles I had been executed by the Parliamentarians in 1649. His reign was characterised by a cultural rebirth following the bleakness and religious conformity of the Cromwellian period. *[National Portrait Gallery, London]*

View of New Park, as developed at the time of Charles II. *[photo from the author's collection]*

his favourite courtesan. Nell was a popular actress at the time of the Restoration, when women began to play female roles – previously played by boys or young men – in the salacious and sexually explicit plays of that period. She proved to be the least greedy of the king's many mistresses, and was also popular with the public for her wit and lack of affectation.

New Park was fenced by Charles II to contain a particular type of red deer that he received as a gift from the king of France, Louis XIV, in 1670. It was then converted into a farm, granted to the Duke of Bedford for 30 years.

Although Charles is frequently remembered for his passion for all the good things in life, he was also a most effective monarch and a patron of the arts and sciences, who presided over a period of great achievements. It is to him that we owe the establishment of the Royal Society among other enduring institutions.

The Park is now used to hold the annual New Forest Show as well as polo matches and other equestrian events.

Christchurch

Although Christchurch is situated outside the New Forest, its history is part of Forest traditions. It is located at the junction of two rivers, the Avon and the Stour, and hence it was a natural port that prompted settlement since prehistoric times. Kathrine Hills, now St Catherine's Hill, was a forest settlement used by the Romans and located a mile or so north of the river junction. As recorded in the Domesday Book, a Saxon town including a priory already existed by the time the Normans arrived.

The Normans developed the priory into a major ecclesiastical site from the moment that Rufus gave the monastery to the famous Flambard (the 'Torch') who was his principal minister. Although Flambard was a Saxon, he became closely associated with the Normans, whom he served faithfully. He was probably as much hated as Rufus himself and is credited with helping the king to impose punitive taxes. Nevertheless, Flambard is responsible for the building of Christchurch Priory and Durham Cathedral, two unique architectural achievements.

Flambard then started demolishing the Saxon church and collecting revenues towards the construction of his new building by the simple expedient of stopping payments to the canons of his newly acquired priory. The death of Rufus, however, upset his plans, because the new king, Henry I, dismissed him and took away his funds. The monastery was passed to the lands of the de Redvers, who were responsible for building a castle, the ruins of which are still visible near the church, most notably the remains of the master's house including a stone chimney. Part of the walls of one of the towers at the top of a steep hillock indicates how large the castle must have been.

Christchurch Priory Church, described as three buildings fused into one. [photo by Pier Paolo Strona]

The Norman fabric inside
Christchurch Church.
[photo by Pier Paolo Strona]

For some reason, Henry thought it wise to have the services of Flambard again and made him Bishop of Durham. By then the funds for Christchurch had disappeared into Henry's coffers, but the de Redvers family supported Flambard financially in his enterprise and eventually they also endowed the priory.

Christchurch has been described as three churches fused into one. The choir was the priory church, but the Norman nave was built as the church of the town, with the subsequent addition of the lady chapel as the church of the lords of the manor.

In spite of this and the resulting confusion of styles, the church has unique features and the overall effect is pleasing. Externally the building is of great length and unrelieved by the expected central tower. The base of such a tower still exists but the structure collapsed in the 13th century destroying the priory church, which was then rebuilt but without the tower.

Brian Vesey-Fitzgerald recounts a well-known story about the church in his book on *Hampshire and the Isle of Wight*:

> Originally the church was intended to be on St Catherine's Hill. But whatever was erected there during the day was found to be cast down during the night and the materials mysteriously transported to a place a mile to the southward. After this had happened several times, it was realized that a church could not be built on the hill, and building was commenced at the site indicated.
>
> Immediately the workers were joined by another. He was a model workman, for he worked all day but was never present when pay was to be drawn nor at meal times. Work progressed apace, and then one day it was found that one of the beams was a foot too short. The strange workman placed his hand upon it, and instantly it fitted – and thereafter the strange workman was seen no more. The carpenter's son had helped to build the church, and so as the workers demanded the church was named Christchurch. The beam is in the church today, projected from a ledge where it has been placed out of the way of initial-cutting visitors.

Wise, in his *The New Forest*, describes the church in the following terms:

The Jesse Screen (1360) in Christchurch Priory Church.
[photo by Pier Paolo Strona]

The church stands at the south-west of the town, on a rising ground between the two rivers, its tower like a seamark to the ships and a landmark to the valley. But the first thing that strikes the visitors is not so much the tower, as the deep, massive north porch, standing right out from the main building, reaching to its roof, with its high-recessed arch, and its rich doorways clearly seen, set between clusters of black Purbeck marble pillars, and ornamented above with a quartz foiled niche.

Standing here, and looking along the north side, the eye rests on the Norman roof of the transept, the low red arches interlacing each other, their spandrils rich with billed and fishscale mouldings; whilst beyond rises the Norman turret, banded with its three strong-courses, and enriched with its arcades, the space between them netted over with coils of twisted cables.

There is the Norman work, such as you can see scarcely anywhere else in England. And imagine what the Church once was, a massive lantern-tower springing up from the midst, the crown of all this beauty.

Soon after its reconstruction in 1150, the new priory was given to the order of the Augustine monks and continued as an important part of the community until its dissolution in 1539. The last prior, John Draper, who is buried within the church, petitioned for the dissolution of the priory and received a generous pension for his efforts. While the church was spared, the cloisters and other buildings were destroyed at that time in accordance with the King Henry VIII's orders.

Highcliffe Castle

Another interesting site to visit along the coast just outside the Forest is Highcliffe Castle. After years of neglect, it has been renovated mainly by the efforts of local volunteers and some money from the Heritage Lottery Fund.

Highcliffe Castle was home to four generations of the Stuart family, the most prominent of whom was Lord Stuart de Rothesay.

The first of them, John Stuart (1713–1792), married Mary, the daughter of Lady Mary Wortley Montagu. A woman of many intellectual accomplishments, Lady Mary was the first to introduce the Turkish practice of inoculation against smallpox into England, demonstrating the techniques on her own children. The method, which involved a series of scratches into which smallpox skin peelings were inserted, became popular around the middle of the 1700s until it was displaced by the vaccination developed by Edward Jenner. Lady Mary's enthusiasm for the Turkish method came from the time when her husband was ambassador to the Sultan's court.

John's successful career was prompted by a casual encounter with Frederick, the Prince of Wales, who entrusted him with the education of his son, the future King George III. The early death of Frederick resulted in John Stuart becoming the advisor of his young protégé, who became King George III on the death of his grandfather in 1760. John Stuart was to hold high office as a result and, having inherited sufficient wealth, he was able to dedicate himself to his favourite pastimes, which included botanical studies. On one of his expeditions into the New Forest, he happened to wander to the place where Highcliffe Castle now stands and was taken by the beautiful view, which encompasses a large part of the English Channel with the Isle of Wight and the Needles in the background.

He built a large residence in 1773, comprising 30 bedrooms, two libraries and a series of rooms including a laboratory and a museum. Upon his death in 1792, the title and inheritance – including Highcliffe – passed to his son Charles, born in 1753, who was to become General Sir Charles Stuart.

Charles joined the army at the early age of 15 and fought with distinction in the American War of Independence, but found it impossible to save the house, which was threatened by the sea continuously eroding the cliff. That was the end of the first Highcliffe house and the land was sold. Charles saw action again in the Mediterranean, where his deputy was General John Moore of La Coruña's fame, and he worked in close collaboration with Horatio Nelson. The career of Sir Charles was cut short by his early death in 1801 at the age of 48.

He was succeeded by his son Charles, who was born in 1779. He was to have a distinguished career as a diplomat serving in Vienna, Paris, St Petersburg and in many other postings and diplomatic missions. He served with distinction during the Napoleonic and post-Napoleonic periods. It was this Charles who became Lord Stuart de Rothesay and was able to buy back the land, in around 1802, which had belonged to his grandfather. The construction of the second Highcliffe mansion, which is the one still standing, began in 1831.

Prior to this, Lord Stuart participated in delicate negotiations regarding the future of Portugal and Brazil. It was a difficult period that saw the exile of the King of Portugal to Brazil and the defeat of his father's deputy, General John Moore, at La Coruña. That critical situation only started to change in Britain's favour in 1809 when Wellington took control of the Peninsular War.

Charles Stuart served during the post-Napoleonic period, as ambassador to the newly established French court ruled by Louis XVIII. This was a period when British foreign policy was dominated by the personality of Lord Castlereagh, whose dramatic suicide in 1822 by cutting his throat with a razor blade surprised and grieved Britain as well as the rest of the world. This led to the return of Canning as Foreign Secretary, under whom Lord Stuart was unable to work. Ironically one of his daughters was to marry Canning's son, Carlo.

In spite of his animosity towards Canning, Stuart was willing to accept his invitation to act as special envoy to the court of Brazil to resolve the problem posed by the independence of that country from Portugal and Portugal's consequent unhappiness about this. Disenchanted with the slow progress of his negotiations and because of his disputes with Canning, he returned to England in 1826.

Following the early death of Canning in 1827, Lord Stuart became ambassador to the French court of Charles X, son of Louis XVIII, whose rule was threatened by the revolution of 1830. The appointment of Lord Palmerston as Foreign Secretary resulted in the recall of Lord Stuart in 1831.

The return to England allowed him to concentrate on the rebuilding of Highcliffe, which he adorned with 16th-century carvings from the Grande Maison des Andelys and others from the 10th-century Benedictine Abbey at Jumièges, now in the Metropolitan Museum of New York. The stained-glass window in the entrance hall was taken from a church at Rouen and tapestry that was displayed in the same hall was said to have belonged to the St John's Knights of Malta. The home was mostly designed by Lord Stuart using the professional services of a young architect and completed in around 1835.

His beautiful and clever daughter Charlotte, married to Carlo – who was to become the first Viceroy of India – died there in 1861. His other daughter, Louisa, an accomplished artist, married Lord Waterford and took possession of Highcliffe upon the death of her father in 1845, a few years after he had been appointed ambassador to Russia.

Neither of the daughters had a child and when Louisa died in 1892, the house passed to a cousin called Charles, who also left no successor.

After several other owners, the property was acquired by the Claretians, a Catholic congregation that converted it into a seminary from 1953 to 1966. They were founded in 1849 in Spain by St Antonio Claret and were dedicated to the cult of St Mary. The diminishing number of young men interested in joining led to its decline and, following the departure of the Claretians, the house fell on bad times. Many of its best features were sold or vandalized and the building caught fire twice. It was only recently that the process of restoration has brought back some of the beautiful features of the building.

Hurst Castle

Hurst Castle is worth a visit. The castle is located at the end of a narrow strip of land composed of pebbles deposited by the currents, which effectively form a breakwater. The distance between Hurst Castle and the Isle of Wight is only a mile and the currents on that stretch of water are very strong.

The position is ideal to defend the western approach to the Solent and Henry VIII built the castle there with stones taken from Beaulieu Abbey.

The site is associated with the unlucky Charles I, who was a prisoner there for 26 days in 1649, during which his fate was being decided.

During the last months of his reign, Charles I left Hampton Court to travel to Hampshire. He stopped first at Twyford Abbey and then went on to the Isle of Wight, seeking the support of its governor, Colonel Hammond. Being a confirmed Parliamentarian, Hammond betrayed Charles I to Cromwell, for which he was handsomely rewarded by Parliament. After staying 13 months on the Isle of Wight, the King was taken to Hurst Castle and from there to London, where he was beheaded.

Sir Thomas Herbert describes the arrival of Charles I at Hurst Castle as follows:

> The wind and tide favouring, the King and his attendants crossed the narrow sea … and landed at Hurst Castle, or Block House rather, effected by order of King Henry VIII, upon a spot of earth a good way into the sea, and joined to the firm land by a narrow neck of sand, which is covered over with small loose

View of Hurst Castle from the narrow strips of gravel connecting it to the mainland. *[photo by Pier Paolo Strona]*

stones and pebbles; and upon both sides the sea beats, so as at spring tides and stormy weather the land passage is formidable and hazardous. The Castle has very thick stone walls, and the platforms are regular, and both have several culverins and sakers mounted … The Captain of this wretched place was not unsuitable; for, at the King's going ashore, he stood ready to receive him with small observance. His look was stern. His hair and beard were black and burly. He held a partisan in his hand; and Switz-like, has a great basket-hilt sword on his side. Hardly could one see a man of more grim aspect, and no less robust and rude was his behaviour.

The castle was used continuously since its construction by Henry VIII until the end of World War II. It is now a museum and can be reached by walking along the narrow strip or taking a small boat from Keyhaven.

Lymington

Lymington is another of the ports to the south of the Forest, which along with Christchurch and Beaulieu, now has negligible trade. However, it was for many years the most important of the New Forest ports. There are no outstanding monastic buildings in Lymington and its church is mainly famous for having been used as a stable by Cromwell's soldiers. The town saw little fighting during the Civil War but there was constant movement of troops because of its harbour.

The most beautiful part of Lymington is its wide main street and the numerous Georgian houses on either side. The Saturday market still takes place here. In the words of Vesey-Fitzgerald:

Lymington lives only on Saturday nights, for on Saturday nights the Forest people come in to do their shopping, and then for some four hours the town is noisy and crowded and exciting – a mixture of market-town and sea-port and fair … All the way down the wide street there are stalls, and the stall-holders

Lymington Quay Lane brings memories of its days as a major port. [photo by Pier Paolo Strona]

View from the Lymington Salterns to the Isle of Wight. Notice the Needles in the centre of the picture. [photo by Pier Paolo Strona]

shout; and some try to bully the passer-by and lookers-on and some try cajoling, and some mix the two in the most bewildering manner.

Its port is now small and mainly used by pleasure boats, but in 1345 it contributed more men and boats than Portsmouth to the fleet marshalled by England for the invasion of France.

At the bottom of the High Street is a lane descending to the port along Quay Hill, with beautiful cottages, many of which are now restaurants and shops.

Lymington originated from part of a land grant given to Richard Redvers by Henry I for supporting him in preference to his older brother Robert, who was on a Crusade to the Holy Land at the time when Rufus was killed. Among those lands was Christchurch and the Isle of Wight.

Richard Redvers's grandson created the town of Lymington in 1184 by subdividing the land into medieval-type allotments, which is still discernible in the narrow frontage of most High Street shops. These plots were five yards (4.6 m) wide and 110 yards (100 m) in depth as that suited the way in which the land was ploughed in those days. Lymington became famous for its market and the economic life of the different traders in the town. From the 12th-century on, it was an important centre for the manufacturing of salt. Seawater was converted into brine in shallow pools, or 'salterns', and the brine was then boiled inside large barns to produce salt. The industry lasted until the early 19th-century and was an important source of revenue for the town as well as the government. By the end of the 18th-century, production reached 5,000 tons per year.

The industry collapsed due to the discovery of salt mines elsewhere and the old salterns became disused. The banks of some of them can still be seen towards the south of the town.

The town became part of the turnpike system in 1765 and a pub called The Tollhouse Inn still exists at the entrance to the town where the tolls were collected. It was as late as 1859 when Lymington was connected to the London to Bournemouth railway by a short branch starting from Brockenhurst. The line was soon extended to a jetty from where a journey to the Isle of Wight could be undertaken.

The arrival of French troops loyal to Louis XVI had a powerful effect on the small town. They were the remnants of the royalist regiments that fought during the French Revolution. These forces participated in the failed invasion of Brittany in 1795 after which many of those who survived returned to Lymington and integrated in the local society.

North of Lymington is an old fort called Buckland Rings, dating from at least the Iron Age. It was also occupiedat the time of the Romans and coins of the period have been found there. It has been called the finest earthwork in the Forest district.

Towards the west you may be able to see a tall construction called Sway Tower and built in concrete. This was the work of Andrew Peterson, born of American

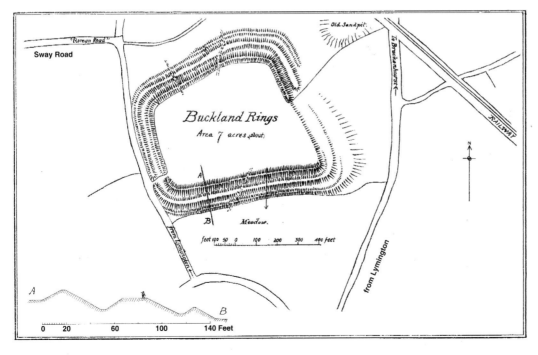

The Buckland Rings encampment is located north of Lymington. It covers an area of around 7 acres (3 Ha) surrounded by three steep banks and two ditches. Notice Sway Road to the North West which was part of an old Roman Road (after Williams-Freeman).

and Dutch parentage, who settled in Sway after his return to England from India, where he had been a High Court judge. Andrew Thomas Turton Peterson lived a colourful life from 1814 to 1906, starting as a young sailor, during which time he took charge of an entire ship during a mutiny. He changed careers later on and eventually became a judge.

Mr Peterson was a firm believer in the properties of concrete, a material not popular in England at that time but which he thought indestructible. He built a spacious country house of that material, to which he later added the Sway Tower, which he finished in 1885 after six years' work. The tower was built without scaffolding by using an ingenious system of moving moulds, and, in spite of signs of wear, it is still an impressive structure.

Mr Peterson was a spiritualist and communicated with a number of spirits, the most important of which were those of the political writer and activist Thomas Paine and Sir Christopher Wren, the architect of St Paul's Cathedral and many other famous buildings. According to Peterson, he began building his tower upon instructions from Wren. Spiritualism was all the rage at the time and towers were seen as a way of communicating more easily with the spirits.

The tower consists of 13 storeys and is 70 metres high, offering breathtaking views. Unfortunately it is no longer open to the public. Peterson became so attached to his folly that his ashes were deposited in a crypt beneath the tower. They were moved to Sway churchyard in 1957 when the tower was sold.

Another interesting religious character at the time was Mary Ann Girling, who was the founder of the New Forest Shakers, a curious religious sect, that like the original group from the US, were driven to dance during their meetings.

She was born in Suffolk in 1827 and died in the New Forest in

1886. Mother Girling was married and had many children of whom only one survived. William, born in 1855, was to accompany her in her mission.

In 1864 she had a vision to leave the world's ways and follow the Lord, receiving the stigmata and claiming to be the female version of Christ, and, as such, the eternal reincarnation of God. She started preaching in her native Suffolk and rapidly formed a group of 50 or so disciples.

The 'Girlingites', as they were known, preached celibacy and lived a communal life being 'brothers' and 'sisters' to each other, with the figure of Mary Ann as their 'mother'. Their services consisted of reading passages from the Bible followed by discussion and prayer. These more conventional parts of the services were followed by dances and trances at the end.

Finding themselves persecuted in Suffolk, the Shakers moved to London before Mary Ann was directed by a vision to go to the New Forest. There, with

The New Forest Lodge in Vaggs Lane nowadays. The Lodge was the home of the Girlingites until their eviction on 15th December 1874 when the bailiffs threw their possessions into the open field opposite the property. *[photo from the author's collection]*

the help of a rich follower and a mortgage, she was able to purchase New Forest Lodge in Vaggs Lane at Hordle. The small mortgage of around 40% of the price of the house was to be their undoing.

The group settling at the Lodge was around 150 strong; their dress was simple, black clothes for the men and white blouses and bloomers for the women. The men worked the land and made shoes in an attempt to achieve economic independence.

It did not take long for the Children of God, as they called themselves, to find enemies in the New Forest, particularly in the shape of a local vicar who was also from Suffolk and an enemy of the sect right from the beginning. He thought that Mary Ann held on to her congregation by 'mesmerizing' them, hypnotism being very popular at that time. For many spiritualists, hypnotism was the proof of the existence of an immortal soul separated from the physical body.

At the sect's peak, Mary Ann invited members of the press and other interested parties to attend the services. Unfortunately their public-relations success was not commensurate with their business sense and they fell behind with their mortgage payments. The mortgagor brought the bailiffs in and some of the livestock was seized. The amount raised at the auction was more than sufficient to pay the overdue interest on the mortgage and the balance could have been used to avoid the forthcoming crisis but nobody paid that money to the community or offered any explanation.

This led to a further default in the mortgage and to an eviction order at the end of 1874 following which 40 sheriff's officers and men threw their possessions onto an open field opposite the property. This happened on 15 December and was followed by a rainy night. Local farmers took pity on them and their children and next morning the 70 or so members still left (some having already deserted the flock) were offered a barn.

The tribulations had just started for the group as the enemies of the sect tried – unsuccessfully – to declare Mary Ann mad to have her imprisoned in a lunatic asylum.

The events of 15 December and the following days were widely reported in the press and resulted in a tide of sympathy for the Shakers. This brought not only immediate financial help but also the support of Auberon Herbert, the third Earl of Caernarvon, who, in spite of his aristocratic background, was a republican and saw himself as a champion of the poor. Herbert was related to William Cowper of Broadlands – the local politician and landowner concerned with social issues – having married his niece Florence in 1871.

Auberon Herbert defended the Shakers, particularly after having found out that New Forest Lodge was sold a week after the eviction for a sum nearly half its original cost. As a final insult, Mary Ann was handed the balance of the auction of their livestock by the sheriff's officers on Christmas Eve! That balance could have been used to pay the interest demanded by the mortgagor that had prompted the eviction of the sect and the sale of the Lodge.

It was through Herbert's office that William Cowper helped the Shakers. William and his wife, Georgina, were spiritualists and played host to many meetings, inviting well-known mediums. One of their many initiatives was to call a Broadlands Conference on Spiritualism, which was held in July 1874, bringing together members of many religious communities including Mary Ann and other unconventional delegates.

Small plaque on the wall of Hordle Church. The only reminder of her and the other twelve Girlingites buried in the Churchyard. *[photo from the author's collection]*

After their eviction, the Shakers intended to take refuge in the barns and tents of Mr Auberon Herbert while Cowper started an appeal to raise money for them.

The Girlingites found that the only solution to their economic problems was to arrange a tour of their temporary accommodation with Mary Ann at its head. (They were already a tourist attraction for the day trippers coming from Bournemouth and Lyndhurst by bus or charabanc.)

The Shakers continued to decrease in number. In

1884 Mary Ann fell ill, with what was later discovered to be cancer of the womb. The members continued to leave, decreasing to only 20 in 1886. On 18 September 1886, Mary Ann died after a long and painful illness. She was 59 years old. She and 12 of the sect members are interred in unmarked graves in Hordle churchyard.

That same year, Auberon Herbert moved to the Old House in Burley. He had just written a remarkable tract called *The Right and Wrong of Compulsion by the State* becoming more radicalized in his fight against the government. His defence of the rights of the individual put him in the fold of the anarchists. He died at the end of 1906 having built a most extraordinary house consisting of a rather unlikely series of different rooms.

Today the New Forest Lodge of the Girlingites is known as Hordle Grange and is a private residence. The converted stable that served as a chapel to the Girlingites is still there.

Boldre

Boldre is another typical New Forest village, still largely unseen by the visitors and consisting of a widely spaced series of secluded houses and cottages.

It has the distinction of being the place where William Gilpin, the author of the famous book *Forest Scenery* was vicar from 1777 until his death in 1807. Reverend Gilpin built a school and a poor house in the village. The former is still standing and is now known as 'Gilpin's Cottage'.

The church at Boldre is of Norman origin but has many recent additions. It is very beautiful and deserves a visit. Wise described the church as follows:

> Its tower stands boldly out, almost away from the church, just between the
> nave and the chancel, serving formerly, like Brockenhurst steeple, as a landmark
> to the Forest; whilst the long outline of the nave is broken only by the south

The Church at Boldre. "Its tower stands boldly out, almost away from the Church". *[photo by Pier Paolo Strona]*

porch, and its three dormer windows. The south aisle is the oldest part, with its three Norman arches arising from square piers, whilst the north aisle is divided from the nave by a row of early-English arches springing from plain black Purbeck marble shafts.

The church of Boldre, like the old one in Brockenhurst, is built away from the village as they were situated in the centre of the parish rather than the centre of the village.

The naturalist W.H. Hudson (1841-1922) was born and raised in Argentina, and came to England at the age of 33. He wrote many books describing birds and animals in his native country as well as in England and had a high regard for the New Forest and the whole of Hampshire. He was way ahead of his time as an early ecologist, lamenting what was happening across the world. He wrote: "The species now being exterminated, not only in South America but everywhere in the globe are, as far as we know, untouched by decadence. They are links in a chain, and branches on the tree of life, with their roots in a past inconceivably remote; and but for our action, they would continue to flourish, reaching outward to an equally distant future, blossoming into higher and more beautiful forms, and gladding innumerable generations of our descendants". (From *The Naturalist in La Plata*.)

William Hudson, the author lived in Boldre in the early 1900s in a house now called Royden Manor. In his book *Hampshire Days* he described the house and its surrounding land as follows:

> The house, too, that gave me shelter must be spoken of; for never have I known any human habitation in a land where people are discovered dwelling in so many secret, green, out-of-date places, which had so much of nature in and about it.

And he goes on to describe the house itself:

> A small picturesque red-brick house with high pitched roof and tall chimneys a great part of it overrun with ivy and creepers, the walls and tiled roof stained by time and many-coloured lichens to a richly variegated greyish red. The date of the house, cut in a stone tablet in one of the rooms, was 1692.

He also wrote a series of books which are still very popular in Argentina, his country of birth. He left it never to return, although he could not forget those early days which he considered to be the best part of his life.

Perhaps the best known of those books is the one entitled *Far away and long ago* in which he narrates the part of his life lived in the Pampas. Theodore Roosevelt in 1916 paid tribute to Hudson's writing by saying:

> He brings before us the wild rider of the Pampas as Gogol brings before us the wild rider of the steppes.

Beaulieu

This is one of the most popular places in the Forest. Beaulieu's name clearly indicates the beauty of the place and it is now a tourist spot attracting many visitors. In the words of Hudson:

> Beaulieu … has a distinction above all Hampshire villages, and is unlike all others in its austere beauty and atmosphere of old-world seclusion and quietude. Above all is that quality which the mind imparts – the expression due to romantic historical associations.

Wise also wrote of Beaulieu in terms that are still relevant to our modern minds:

> Surely there is some profit to be had in coming to a quiet village like this. It will only give us some glimpses of a life which stands out in such strong contrast to our own.

It was, in the Middle Ages, the site of one of the largest abbeys in England, of which little remains. Beaulieu was also the only abbey founded by King John at

A view of Beaulieu, with the pond used to operate a tidal power mill.
[photo from the author's collection]

the request of the Cistercian monks. It is said that this was as a consequence of a dream that King John had and that it was inspired by God. It seems more probable that the reasons for the foundation of the Abbey were political, in so far as the Cistercian order was independent of the rest of the clergy and proved to be a formidable champion of King John during his quarrels with Rome. Whatever the reason, the abbey was constructed in the staggeringly short period of 45 years, by which time King John had died. Some of the stones to build the abbey were quarried in the Isle of Wight and possibly bought into Beaulieu by boat, as well as others from Rouen. However, Vesey-Fitzgerald, amongst others, believed that a causeway still existed then between the Isle of Wight and the mainland at Lepe at neap tides.

A view of Palace House in Beaulieu, originally the gatehouse of the Abbey. *[photo by Pier Paolo Strona]*

In 1538 Henry VIII dissolved the monastery at Beaulieu and sold the land to Thomas Wriothesley, 1st Earl of Southampton, friend and patron of Shakespeare. The Earl was a lawyer by profession and had extensive lands elsewhere. He is one of the best recorded examples of how rewarding the Bar can be!

Following the Dissolution of the Monasteries, most of the abbey was destroyed and its stones used to build the defences at Hurst and Calshot Castles, amongst others. The only original parts of the main abbey that remain are the Lay Brothers' house, which is now a visitors' centre and museum, and the parish church, which was the refectory of the abbey. Palace House, the residence of Lord Montagu, the present owner, was the inner gatehouse of the abbey. The outer gatehouse and a section of the wall, which surrounded the abbey, still remain.

Buckler's Hard

Nearby is Buckler's Hard, which is also of historic interest and is most picturesque. Ships were built here for nearly 100 years and launched directly onto the Beaulieu river. The port was established by John Montagu, 2nd Duke of Montagu, in 1722 and originally intended to be a trading port, with the name of 'Montagu Town', rather than a shipyard. The idea was to process there the sugar that the duke planned to grow on the West Indies islands of St Lucia and St Vincent, given to him by George I. The war with the French foiled this attempt and the duke decided to build ships instead, eventually appointing Henry Adams as Master Builder in 1749, a tradition that continued with his sons. At its height there were five slipways and around 20 cottages. Only two rows of cottages now remain with a broad village street separating them and sloping towards the river. (So broad is the street that many visitors think that the slipways were situated on it.) At the end of one row stands a hotel, which was the master builder's house, and one of the builders' cottages is now a tiny chapel. An excellent display at the entrance of the village describes the activities that took place.

Many fine wooden ships were built there including the famous *Agamemnon*, commanded by Nelson during the siege of Calvi, in which he lost the vision of his right eye. (The ship was lost in Maldonado Bay on the River Plate in 1809, its hull pierced by its own anchor.) This ship, together with *Swiftsure* and *Euryalus*, all built at Buckler's Hard, took part in the Battle of Trafalgar. A.J. Holland pointed out that Buckler's Hard was a major shipbuilding centre, with 53 ships being launched there from 1740 to 1820, which compares favourably with 47 built at Southampton during the same period.

In 1818 the construction of ships ceased, mainly as a consequence of the enterprise having over-extended itself. Adams had contracted to build four ships simultaneously but was unable to deliver them on time to the navy, and the resulting fines and litigation destroyed the business.

Park Hill

Returning towards Lyndhurst along the B3056 road one crosses the railway track before arriving at Park Hill, now a country hotel.

The railway station at the crossing is called Beaulieu Road and one can see there the corrals where pony sales take place.

Progressing along the road one finds the entrance to Park Hill on the left, half-way between the railway station and Lyndhurst. This was the original Old Park set up by the Crown around Lyndhurst, before New Park was established. It originated as a Royal Park because of its deer and was in existence at the time of Edward I; its old boundaries, which are still visible as parts of the embankment, have survived.

It is interesting to note that the two main roads from Salisbury to Beaulieu and Lymington to Southampton used to intercept approximately at the centre of this park. This junction is now situated in the middle of Lyndhurst and causes a serious traffic problem.

At one time the main road from Lymington to Southampton did not follow the route of the current A337, but bent to the right before coming to New Park as there was a lake there. The road continued to Park Hill and passed near our Ashurst Lodge to join the current A35 road to Southampton at the place where the Ashurst (New Forest) railway station is now. This road was called the Cock Road, cock meaning 'main' or the Saltway Road as it was used to carry the salt from the salterns of Lymington. Most probably it was a saltway since pre-Roman times until the collapse of the industry at the beginning of the 19th century.

In 1319 Old Park is recorded as being the property of the Queen Consort of Edward II, Queen Isabella, and in 1331 it became that of Queen Philippa, wife of Edward III.

From then on the park seems to have fallen into a state of neglect, until it was eventually abandoned by the sovereign when New Park was established by Charles II.

Viw of Park Hill from the gardens, now an outstanding hotel. *[photo from the author's collection]*

The land was leased by the Crown to different tenants, until we see it in the hands of Charles Sturgeon at the beginning of the 1800s. Jackman pointed out that Sturgeon's mother "was a lady in her own right, but she married her footman and so dropped that title. They have a servant whose son had the property when Mr Sturgeon died." This was a Mr Tate, who then sold Park Hill to Captain William Morant, famous as the Master of the New Forest Hounds, and who made considerable improvements to the property.

After a new change of ownership, the house was leased to Canon Willingham Rawnsley, who set up a school for gentlemen on the premises. Canon Rawnsley was related to the co-founder of the Council for the Preservation of Rural England and of the National Trust. The school is reputed to have had Thomas Stearns (T.S.) Eliot (1888–1965), the famous poet, as a master. Eliot was born in St Louis, Missouri, and became a British citizen in 1927. He was awarded a Nobel Prize for Literature in 1948.

Canon Rawnsley left the school in 1902 and the new master was Mr Charles E. Ridout. One of the teachers at that time was A.F. Tschiffely, a colourful adventurer of Swiss origin who is closely connected to Argentina, where part of his family lived for several generations. Tschiffely is best remembered for a series of books on his trips in South America, especially the trek he undertook with two Patagonian horses from the Pampas to New York, where he was received as a hero. A result of this trip was a delightful book called *Tschiffely's Ride* and a children's version, *The Tale of Two Horses*, which was a favourite of my generation.

Tschiffely has left a description of Park Hill School in his book Bohemian Junction:

> I had the good fortune later to be transferred to Park Hill, an expensive and therefore exclusive Preparatory School near Lyndhurst, in the New Forest. Thirty five was the maximum number of pupils the school ever had in the course of one term, and among them there were several Princes; and the others were the sons of wealthy social and political figures. The buildings and surrounding parks were old and stately, and my work light and pleasant.

A. F. Tschiffely was born in Switzerland in 1895 but became a school teacher in England where he taught at the New Forest School of Canon Rawnsley. His love of horses led him to Argentina from where he made an epic 10,000mile (16,000 km) journey, riding two horses from Buenos Aires to New York. A friendly and kindly man, he felt equally at home with the roughest gaucho as with the lords of the land. His books also reflect unusual awareness of human wrongs and a desire for social justice.

During Tschiffely's time the school buildings were spacious and he had at his disposal two large and beautifully furnished rooms, besides a study filled with books. He was a keen horseman, as demonstrated by his subsequent American feat. He wrote:

> One of my great joys was riding through the beautiful New Forest, where at different times I saw a vagabond-like, bearded man. Friends who knew him informed me that he was W.H. Hudson, a naturalist and bird-watcher.

Tschiffely later became a great admirer of Hudson as he started to develop an interest in the Argentine Pampas and its inhabitants.

Park Hill School had to close at the beginning of World War I and amalgamated with the Priory, another preparatory school in Malvern. The closure of the school was followed by the sale of Park Hill to Sir Stephen Lund, who improved the property before he died in 1926, when it was bought by Colonel Hargreaves and turned into a hotel.

During World War II the house was requisitioned by Southampton Fire Brigade, who responded from there to the fires caused by the frequent bombing of the town. An ex-fireman visiting the hotel many years afterwards confirmed the previous use of the premises, and provided the interesting piece of information that he had been in charge of looking after the messenger pigeons.

The house reverted to its use as a hotel after the war. The beauty of the surroundings, the tranquillity, the friendly service and the excellent cuisine make this one of the most pleasant hotels in our part of the country.

Ashurst Lodge

Ashurst Lodge can be reached by a private road from the A35. Between the A35 and the entrance of the Lodge a large saltpetre factory existed.

Nothing is known of the early history of Ashurst Lodge, but it is reasonable to assume that some early habitation may have existed there because of its excellent position on high ground and near a stream. Some remains of Roman pottery have been found nearby. In addition, an important track connecting Lymington to Southampton ran close by.

The site of the saltpetre works is associated with the origins of the Lodge through a colourful entrepreneur called Cornelius Stephinson, a native of Liège who, in the 1560s, took refuge in England, as did many of his Protestant fellow countrymen. Cornelius had the expertise required to produce a series of chemical compounds, in particular saltpetre, which, together with sulfur and coal, is one of the ingredients of gunpowder, of great strategic value during the reign of Elizabeth I.

At that time the political stability of England had profoundly altered following Henry VIII's break with the Catholic Church in 1533. His marriage to Anne Boleyn, following his divorce from Catherine of Aragon, had incurred the ire of Rome and led to his excommunication. The situation was to improve during the

Trace of a map from the Select
Committee of Woods and Works
showing Ashurst Lodge and the
Banks of the Saltpetre works, now
half way along the access road to the
Lodge. Notice the New Forest Union
plot next to the Lyndhurst Road
Station, now called Ashurst New
Forest Station. The New Forest Union
was the name of the Workhouse for
the region, now a hospital.

93

brief reign of his devout Catholic daughter, Mary, whose marriage to Philip II of Spain – conducted incidentally in Winchester Cathedral – heralded a period of peace and stability. The early death of Mary led to her Protestant half-sister, Elizabeth, becoming Queen; she was promptly excommunicated by the Pope who went as far as to encourage her assassination.

The resulting threat to England from her Catholic brother-in-law, Philip II, was to culminate in the ill-fated attack by the 'Invincible' Armada in 1588, and led Elizabeth to give further support to the revolt then taking place in the Flemish States against Spanish rule.

It was thus imperative for Elizabeth to create a strong and self-sufficient military. When she came to the throne in 1558, England imported its saltpetre from the Continent as nobody here knew how to manufacture it. She adopted the policy of encouraging Protestant refugees, such as Stephinson, who had special skills, to settle in her domains.

Cornelius started by refining alum and copper, when working in Dorset. The enterprise did not prosper and in 1576 he petitioned the Queen for a grant of 400 acres (160 ha) in the New Forest in which to manufacture saltpetre, with the production of 40 tons a year to be purchased by the Crown. The concession was granted together with the permission to collect the nitrite-rich soils in neighbouring farms as raw material, with the assistance of the Justices of the Peace if required. The fuel needed, including branches, turf and heath, was to be gathered within his 400 acres. A further condition stipulated that he was only allowed to build on the land a single dwelling house for his family and servants, in addition to the saltpetre factory.

The foundations of his saltpetre works are still clearly visible halfway between the main road and the entrance to the Lodge. The remains of the rectangular embankment measure approximately 150 m long by 50 m wide, and it is one of the earliest saltpetre factories in the whole country. The dwelling house of Cornelius stood in what are now the grounds of Ashurst Lodge, probably in the same position as the central core of the present main building.

In spite of his expertise, Cornelius was unable to produce saltpetre in suffi-ciently large quantities and the resulting financial problems, coupled with the failure of the previous enterprise in Dosert, forced him to abandon the Ashurst works. By the middle of 1584 the Exchequer ordered the 400-acre enclosure to be returned to open forest.

From then on a series of Forest Keepers took up residence in the Lodge. Gilpin wrote in 1794 that there were 15 walks, or divisions, in the Forest, each with its lodge, and added:

> A few of those Lodges are elegant mansions; and are the habitations of the
> Keepers, who are generally men of fashion, or fortune.

What is left of the foundation of the Saltpetre works still clearly visible when driving along the entrance road to the Lodge. *[photo by Keith Godwin]*

95

A round barrow in the proximity of Ashurst Lodge. *[photo by Keith Godwin]*

Ashurst was one of those walks supervised by a Keeper whose job was mainly a sinecure given by the king. The Keepers treated the land occupied by the lodges as their own private property and obtained considerable profits from exploiting their own walks.

The period from 1583 to 1854 saw a series of Keepers living at the Lodge, many of whom would seem to have been very active in exploiting the Forest for their own ends. In 1708, during the tenancy of Robert Nixon, Ashurst Lodge was burnt to the ground, together with its outhouses and stables. It needed to be completely rebuilt this time in brick, which was in fashion following the Great Fire of London of 1667.

William Rooke was Keeper at the Lodge in 1741 and soon after moved to a disputed area adjacent to the Burley Bailiwick where he murdered one of the Keepers in an argument arising over the killing of a deer. Rooke and his men, probably prompted by the then Lord Warden, the Duke of Bedford, confronted another group of keepers from the Burley Bailiwick hunting in a disputed walk. The man in possession of that Bailiwick was then the Marquis of Winchester, whose lands, while still part of the Forest, were not under the authority of the Lord Warden, who resented this anomaly. In spite of his crime and the subsequent sentence, Rooke lived in freedom to die of natural causes under the protection of the Duke of Bedford.

George Maynard was another Keeper at Ashurst, from 1782 to 1827, during which time he helped to improve the surrounding grounds and added a meadow to the property. His grandson, also George Maynard, became the next Keeper from 1827 until 1863 or 1864. This was a time of great change in the Forest, following the Deer Removal Act and a series of Enclosure Acts. In 1846 the London and South Western Railway came to the Forest, cutting through the grounds of Ashurst Lodge.

The Lodge itself is much older than the adjoining village to which it gave its name. The village grew beside the railway station that the residents of Lyndhurst refused to have in their village, i.e. Lyndhurst Road station, which in 1995 changed its name to Ashurst (New Forest) station.

Later the Lodge was to become the residence of the Assistant Deputy Surveyor. This was an important position following the abolition of the Lord Warden's office and its replacement by the Deputy Surveyor, appointed by the Office of Woods.

View of one of the Work houses in Ashurst, now converted into a hospital. Located next to the railway station, they served several New Forest towns and were the starting of the present-day village. *[photo by Pier Paolo Strona]*

The first of these Assistant Deputy Surveyors, Colonel William Reed, who served the Crown for more than 30 years, lived in the Lodge from 1854 to 1880. He was very efficient and highly regarded. A set of Victorian iron gates at the entrance to Lyndhurst churchyard were donated in his memory, although he is buried in Brockenhurst. Gerald Lascelles, the most well known of the Deputy Surveyors (1880–1914) was to lament his passing even though he had not been in office a month at the time of William Reed's death.

Reed's assistant, James Roberts, was then appointed Assistant Deputy Surveyor and held the office from 1881 to 1902. Ashurst Lodge benefited from the new appointment as James had been trained as an architect and undertook a substantial amount of building work in the Forest. One of his earliest assignments was the enlargement of the Lodge in 1881.

The earliest surviving plans of Ashurst Lodge, dated 1784, show it as a rectangular building of approximately 26 ft by 43 ft in plan (8 m by 13 m) with a small porch and an attached wash house. These dimensions agree with the central and older portion of the existing building. By 1853, a dairy had been added to the ground floor with a cellar below; the latter was recorded as early as 1781 and it is still there.

These changes were reported in the 1853 survey of the Forest Lodges, which also mentions that Ashurst Lodge had three rooms on the ground floor, four bedrooms upstairs and two other on the top floor. The 1881 additions of James Roberts had to have been substantial, judging from the outline shown on the Ordnance Survey map of 1898.

The last of the surveyors living at Ashurst Lodge was John Henry Dixon (from 1902 to 1919), who remained there throughout World War I. His departure in 1919 marked the end of an era, as Ashurst Lodge then ceased to be used by the Forest officers. The Lodge became the residence of the Crum-Ewing family from the beginning of 1921 when two new wings were added. During World War II it was requisitioned, as were most large houses in the Forest.

Fred Bennett lived in the gatehouse of the Lodge throughout the war years

View of the Wessex Institute's main building at Ashurst Lodge. Towards the right, a new extension. [photo by Keith Godwin]

and remembered that the first contingent of troops to arrive there were issued with Churchill tanks. According to the official records, those vehicles seem to have been issued to the Canadian Calgary Armoured Regiment, which fought with distinction throughout the war. Although none of these soldiers was quartered in the Lodge itself, the billets spread between the existing drive and the nearby railway tracks. They were to load their tanks and other vehicles on flat train wagons to leave early one morning and take part in the ill-fated Dieppe Raid of 19 August 1942. Railway sidings then existed on what is now a camp site near Ashurst Lodge, which also contained a sawmill operated by Italian prisoners of war, moved there from a camp near Brockenhurst.

Ashurst Lodge also played an important part in the planning of the Normandy invasion. Mr B. Stannard once revisited the Lodge, where he was posted as a driver to the HQ of the 6th Port Construction and Repair Group of the Royal Engineers, who moved into Ashurst Lodge in July 1943. The purpose of the group was to build a military port at Marchwood which was to play a major part in D-Day and where some of the sections for the Mulberry Harbour were erected. The group had a total of more than thousand men living in

Southampton and grouped in three different companies. The whole of the group had to be transported by tram every day from the Common to the quay, from where they took a ferry to Marchwood. Lt Col Bertlin was flown in from the Middle East on Churchill's orders to head it. The Mulberry Harbour was composed of large floating concrete caissons that the invasion force was to take with them to Normandy to create a port. The task allocated to Bertlin was not only to construct Marchwood Military Port but also to oversee the construction of the Mulberry Harbour units and to erect the pumping station for the PLUTO (pipeline under the ocean) project that was to provide the fuel essential for the advance of the armies into Normandy. Ashurst Lodge became the headquarters of the group with the officers and a team of surveyors living in the main Lodge, and the support staff, including Stannard, in the outer buildings. The whole project took only one year to be completed, from June 1943 to June 1944. They left the Lodge after D-Day in September 1944 and sailed to Normandy in landing craft.

Next to move into the Lodge were friendly American troops, who got along well with the local residents, whom they invited to cinema shows and concerts in an area cleared next to our access road. The records seem to indicate that they were a company of the 1302 Engineering General Service Regiment, which

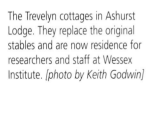

The Trevelyn cottages in Ashurst Lodge. They replace the original stables and are now residence for researchers and staff at Wessex Institute. *[photo by Keith Godwin]*

crossed to France at the beginning of 1945 and were disbanded a year or so later. These soldiers were displaced by black American troops, who belonged to the 14th Ports Group and worked by day in the docks in Southampton. They were vital to the war effort as they handled most of the supplies for the Allied forces fighting on the Continent. They also made many friends among the local population.

After the war, Ashurst Lodge was returned to Mr Crum-Ewing, who died shortly after. His daughter, who had married into the wealthy Hamilton family, owners of vast estates in Scotland, chose not to live at the Lodge, which was then taken over by Hampshire County Council and turned into an old people's home. Computational Mechanics International moved to the premises in 1982 and since then the group has continued to develop the premises in a sympathetic manner. Four years later saw the launch of the Wessex Institute of Technology (WIT), which is now a research centre with an international reputation. Harold Newman, reporting in *Hampshire Magazine*, has written:

> The 'Lodge' stood before me across an immaculate lawn bounded by a natural
> growth of ancient oaks. Small cottages blended naturally with their mother
> Lodge and tucked neatly to the rear was the necessary car park thoughtfully
> sheltered amidst shrubbery and flower beds. It was difficult to accept that I had
> entered the domain of High Technology …

WIT was established to act as a link between academia and industry. It was based on our conviction that there was a need to set up a new type of centre to communicate effectively with industry. The initiative has now developed into a successful institution. In the words of Harold Newman:

> Here in the heart of rural Hampshire it is difficult to appreciate that there exists
> a group of people engaged in and committed to work of world class impor-
> tance, aimed at making far better lives for all of us. The beauty of it is that in
> their work there is no environmentally unfriendly side-product such as noise,
> vibration or pollution of any kind, it is all done by computer.

BIBLIOGRAPHY

ALONSO, R. (Editor), Juan *Manuel de Rosas. Cartas del Exilio 1853/1875*, Rodolfo Alonso Editor S.R.L., Buenos Aires, 1974.

BENNETT, F., Private communication, 1977.

COATES, Richard, *Hampshire Place Names*, Ensign Publications, Southampton, 1993.

COBBETT, W., *Rural Rides*, London, 1826.

COCHRANE, Charles, Early Roads in the New Forest, *Hampshire Magazine*, May 1970.

CORNISH, C.J., *The New Forest and the Isle of Wight*, Seeley & Co., London, 1985.

CUNLIFFE, Barry (Editor), *Heywood Sumner's Wessex*, Roy Gasson Associates, Wimborne, Dorset, 1985.

DE CRESPIGNY, Rose and HUTCHINSON, Horace, *The New Forest: Its Tradition, Inhabitants and Customs*, John Murray, 1895.

FRANKLIN, R., *Lord Stuart of Rothesay,* Images Publishing Ltd, Upton-upon-Severn, 1993.

GILPIN, William, *Remarks on Forest Scenery and other Woodland Views*, R. Blamire, London, Second edition, 1794.

HARDCASTLE, F., *Records of Burley: aspects of a New Forest village*, Chameleon International, Spalding, Revised edition, 1989.

HEATHCOTE, Terry, *A Wild Heritage. The History and Nature of the New Forest*, Ensign Publications, Southampton, 1990.

HERBERT, Sir Thomas, *Memoirs of the Two Last Years of the Reign of King Charles I*, 1702.

HIRSCH, Pam, *Barbara Leigh Smith Bodichon*, Chatto & Windus, London, 1998.

HOARE, Philip, *England's Lost Eden*, Harper Perennial, London, 2006.

HOLLAND, A.J., *Buckler's Hard. A Rural Shipbuilding Centre*, Kenneth Mason Publications Ltd., Emsworth, Hants, 1993.

HOLMES, Edric, *Wanderings in Wessex*, Robert Scott, London, undated.

HUDSON, W.H., *Hampshire Days*, Longmans, Green & Co., London, 1903.

HUDSON, W.H., *Far away and long ago*, J.M. Dent and Sons Ltd, London, 1918.

HUDSON, W.H., *The Naturalist in La Plata*, J.M. Dent Sons Ltd, London, 1929.

HUXLEY, E., *Florence Nightingale*, Purnell Book Services, London, 1975.

INGS, S.J., *Powder and Prayer. The unique story of a New Forest church and its links with a gunpowder factory.* Published by S.J. Ings in association with Fritham Free Church, Southampton, 2004.

JACKMAN, R., *The story of Park Hill as taken from old books and documents*, private communication, 1975.

JAMES, Jude, *Lymington: A History and Celebration of the Town*, The Francis Frith Collection, Salisbury, 2005.

JAMES, Lawrence, *Raj: The Making and Unmaking of British India*, Little, Brown and Co., London, 1997.

KENCHINGTON, F.E., *The Commoners' New Forest*, Hutchinson Co., London, 1942.

LASCELLES, Gerald, *Thirty-Five Years in the New Forest*, E. Arnold, London, 1915.

LEEK, Sybil, *Diary of a Witch*, Lesley Frewin Publishers Ltd, London, 1975.

LLOYD, A.T., *The Shakers of Hordle*, Hampshire Magazine.

LYNCH, John, *Argentine Dictator. Juan Manuel de Rosas, 1829–1852*, Clarendon Press, Oxford, 1981.

McWILLIAMS TULLBERG, Rita, *Women at Cambridge*, Cambridge University Press, Cambridge, 1998.

MANN, John Edgar, *Hampshire Customs, Curiosities and Country Lore*, Ensign Publications, Southampton, 1994.

MURRAY, Nicholas, *A Life of Matthew Arnold*, Hodder & Stoughton, London, 1996.

NEWMAN, Harold, *The Wessex Institute of Technology – at Home in the New Forest*, Hampshire Magazine, October 1995, pp.32–33.

PASMORE, A. (Editor), *New Forest Explosives*, Hampshire Field Club and Archaeological Society, 1993.

REEVES, R.P., *The History of Ashurst Lodge, 1577–1921*, private communication, 2003.

REEVES, R.P. (Editor), *Use and Abuse of a Forest Resource, New Forest Documents 1632–1700*, New Forest Museum and Library, Lyndhurst, 2006.

Ringwood Official Tour Guide. Published by Ringwood Town Council, 1995.

ROBERTS, P., *Ashurst: A New Forest Railway Village, 1789–1939*, Nova Foresta Publishing, Ashurst, 1995.

ROBERTS, P. (Editor), *Ruin and Reform, New Forest Administrators, 1739–1769*, New Forest Museum and Library, Lyndhurst, 2006.

SALSBURY, Harry, *Highcliffe Castle and the Claretians 1953–1966*, Natula Publications, Christchurch, 2000.

SIBLEY, Patricia & FLETCHER, Robin, *Discovering the New Forest*, Hale, London, 1986.

STAGG, D.J. (Editor), *A Calendar of New Forest Documents: fifteenth to the seventeenth centuries*, Hampshire County Council, 1983.

STAGG, D.J. (Editor), *A Calendar of New Forest Documents, 1244–1334*, Hampshire County Council, 1979.

STANNARD, B., Private communication, 2000.

SUMNER, Heywood, *The New Forest*, 1924; Third Edition, The Dolphin Press, 1972.

SUTHERLAND, G., *Faith, Duty and the Power of Mind: the Cloughs and their circle 1820–1960*, Cambridge University Press, 2006.

TATE, Peter, *The New Forest: 900 Years After*, Macdonald and Jane, London, 1979.

TSCHIFFELY, A.F., *Bohemia Junction*, Hodder & Stoughton, London, 1950.

TUCKER, Jenny, *Burley: A Brief History*, Julians Press, Wimborne, Dorset, undated.

Various Contributors, *The New Forest*, Galley Press, London, 1960.

VESEY-FITZGERALD, B., *Hampshire and the Isle of Wight*, Hale, London, 1949.

WATKIN, D., *The Architecture of Basil Champneys*, Newnham College, Cambridge, 1989.

WILLIAMS-FREEMAN, J.P, *An Introduction to Field Archaeology: As Illustrated by Hampshire*, Macmillan and Co., London, 1915.

WISE, John, *The New Forest: its History and its Scenery*, Gibbings, London, 1862.

APPENDIX

English Monarchs from the Norman Conquest to the Present Day

Normans

William I (the Conqueror)	1066–1087
William II (Rufus)	1087–1100
Henry I	1100–1135
Stephen	1135–1154

Plantagenets

Henry II	1154–1189
Richard I	1189–1199
John	1199–1216
Henry III	1216–1272
Edward I	1272–1307
Edward II	1307–1327 (deposed)
Edward III	1327–1377
Richard II	1377–1399 (deposed)
Henry IV	1399–1413
Henry V	1413–1422
Henry VI	1422–1461 (deposed)

Henry IV, Henry V, Henry VI } House of Lancaster

Edward IV	1461–1483	⎫
Edward V	1483–1483	⎬ House of York
Richard III	1483–1485	⎭

Tudors

Henry VII	1485–1509
Henry VIII	1509–1547
Edward VI	1547–1553
Jane	1553–1553 (lasted only 9 days)
Mary I	1553–1558
Elizabeth I	1558–1603

Stuarts

James I	1603–1625
Charles I	1625–1649 (beheaded)

Commonwealth

Oliver Cromwell	1653–1658 (Lord Protector)
Richard Cromwell	1658–1659 (Lord Protector)

Stuarts Restoration

Charles II	1660–1685
James II	1685–1688 (deposed)

Interregnum (without King) 11 December 1688 to 13 February 1689. This period is sometimes called the Glorious Revolution.

Continuation of the Stuarts

William II and Mary II	1689–1694
William III	1664–1702
Anne	1702–1714

House of Hanover

George I	1714–1727
George II	1727–1760
George III	1760–1820
George IV	1820–1830
William IV	1830–1837
Victoria	1837–1901

House of Saxe-Coburg-Gotha, later Windsor

Edward VII	1901–1910

(Name changed to **House of Windsor** in 1917)

George V	1910–1936
Edward VIII	1936 (abdicated)
George VI	1936–1952
Elizabeth II	1952–

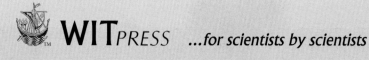

Patagonia, a Forgotten Land

From Magellan to Peron

C.A. BREBBIA, *Wessex Institute of Technology, UK*

This book describes the history of Patagonia from its discovery by Magellan to recent times. Since its early exploration Patagonia has been associated with conditions of extreme hardship and suffering. Men and ships were lost in the dangerous waters of the Straits of Tierra del Fuego, giving rise to tales of mysterious cities populated by the shipwrecked sailors of the many failed expeditions.

Early Spanish attempts to colonize Patagonia also ended in failure and the region remained largely uninhabited until the arrival of the Welsh in 1865. Their peaceful coexistence with the natives ended abruptly when the Argentine Army entered Patagonia and took over the Indian lands, which were promptly distributed to new settlers.

As a new and anarchic society, Patagonia could not fail to attract its share of desperados and adventurers, the most notorious of which are described in the book, including gold prospectors, hunters and bandits such as Butch Cassidy and the Sundance Kid.

The volume also relates the anarchist's struggles that took place in Patagonia at the beginning of the 1900s and the failed attempt by Peron's government to convert Argentina to a nuclear power.

The book conveys the image of Patagonia as still a largely unknown and forbidding place. Five hundred years of recorded history have not dispelled the image of Patagonia being a new frontier.

Contents: EARLY HOPES AND TRIBULATIONS – Magellan, A man of destiny; More ill fated expeditions; Enter Drake; Enter the British, follow the Dutch; IN SEARCH OF DREAMS – The laboratory of mankind; The extraordinary trip of Musters; The city of the Cesares; The man who would be king; CLAIMING THE LAND – Convicts and Adventures, the story of Punta Arenas; Little Wales across the sea; THE CONQUEST OF SOULS – The Falkland/Malvinas dispute; The Patagonia Missionary Society; The visions of Don Bosco; CONQUERING THE WILDERNESS – The Indian wars; The young explorers; EXILES, ADVENTURERS AND OUTLAWS – The Argentine Australia; The gold rush and the story of Popper; The desperadoes; THE FURIOUS AND THE FOOLISH – The anarchists of Patagonia; Its atomic secret.

ISBN: 978-1-84564-061-3

Published 2007, 384pp
£33.00/US$59.00/€49.50

Tradition Today

Edited by: **R. ADAM**, *Robert Adam Architects, UK* and **M. HARDY**, *INTBAU, London, UK*

In January 2002, after a two year gestation period, the International Network for Traditional Buildings, Architecture and Urbanism (INTBAU) was launched. To celebrate the launch, a conference was held to debate the place of tradition in modern society. While INTBAU was specifically concerned with building and urbanism, if tradition was indeed relevant then it must have a place throughout society. The conference forms the basis of this book.

It is an important feature of traditions that they adapt and change. So, while change accelerates so should the adaptation of traditions. If we rely on tradition for the transmission of culture, then the adaptation of traditions is a matter of importance to all of us. If change occurs without the transmission of culture, then culture itself dies; culture cannot be created anew every day. The evolutionary nature of tradition is something often ignored by supporters and opponents alike. It is important that history – that which measures our distance from the past – is not confused with tradition – the past living through us.

The papers presented in this book discuss these points and many others are a fascinating miscellany. With contributions ranging from the practical to the academic these papers can leave no doubt about the continued role and significance of tradition, the passion of those who understand its relevance and the dangers inherent in its denial.

ISBN: 978-1-84564-066-8

Published 2008, 160pp
£29.50/US$59.00/€44.50

Find us at
http://www.witpress.com

Save 10% when you order from our encrypted ordering service in the web using your credit card.

WITPress
Ashurst Lodge, Ashurst, Southampton, SO40 7AA, UK.
Tel: 44 (0) 238 029 3223
Fax: 44 (0) 238 029 2853
E-Mail: marketing@witpress.com